THE APALACHE CHRONICLES

An Englishman's Remarkable Journey

through the Southern Highlands

1653

Excerpts from

The History of the Caribby-Islands

Book II

by Charles de Rochefort

Introduction and Notes by

Richard L. Thornton

Editing and Research by

Marilyn A. Rae

ANCIENT CYPRESS PRESS

Fort Lauderdale

Ancient Cypress Press
Fort Lauderdale
Florida, USA
www.ancientcypresspress.com

ISBN: 978-0-9889648-5-3

Cover illustration by Mary Rae

CONTENTS

INTRODUCTION

HISTOIRE
NATURELLE & MORALE
des
Iles Antilles de
l'Amerique

A ROTTERDAM,
Chez Arnout Leers, Marchant Libraire, 1658.

Charles de Rochefort, ce 26 Aoust 1658
cy devant ministre de s. Euangile en l'Amerique.

THE APALACHE CHRONICLES

8

Cities of Gold

The Appalachian Mountains . . . ancient, mysterious, breathtakingly beautiful . . . a complex landscape of dense vegetation, composed of a seemingly infinite number of species; slopes covered with flowers and ravines choked with rhododendron thickets; gushing streams everywhere; hundreds of waterfalls, hidden coves, boulders, intermittent rock outcrops, earthen mounds on the sites of long abandoned Native American towns; and yet, these mountains are apparently named after a Native American tribe that once lived in the Florida Panhandle. The Apalachee towns were a minimum of 275 miles away from the Appalachian Mountains. This apparent conundrum was explained away by late 20th century historians and anthropologists as a naïve mistake by some 16th century French colonists, but was it?

The Mountain Apalache

The "Kingdom" of Mountain Apalache was actually the progenitor of the Creek Indian Confederacy and the original name for the Creek Indians.[1] Apalache was probably never a true kingdom as De Rochefort labeled it, but more like the organization of the United States before the Constitution was adopted. However, in the later part of the chapter on Apalache, De Rochefort mentioned that provinces had become semi-independent because of the cultural stresses caused by European colonization. There is substantial evidence from the book that Mediterranean or European immigrants played a role in its functioning in later years.

Archaeological and archival evidence suggests that Apalache became a "big time player" after the de Soto Expedition passed through the region in 1540. The Kusa Confederacy, a longtime enemy of the Apalache, collapsed between 1585 and 1600. The original capital, now under Carters Lake, GA, had over 3,000 houses, but was completely abandoned during this period. A smaller capital was established around 1600 AD, 126 miles downstream near present day Childersburg, AL. Etowah Mounds was also abandoned then. For many decades archaeologists thought it was permanently abandoned, but recent ground radar studies have identified a later occupation by an unknown ethnic group. The capital of Apalache was *probably* moved at this time northward into the Nottely River Valley in Union County, GA to be at the center of its new territory.

The original Apalache province in the late 1500s occupied the north-central Georgia Piedmont and most southerly ranges of the Blue Ridge Mountains. It is mentioned in several Spanish, French and Creek Indian archives. To the north of the Apalache were the Itsate, descendants of Itza Maya immigrants, who arrived in Georgia in the period between the destruction of Palenque by a volcano, c. 800 AD, and around 1050 AD when the climate in southern Mexico began to improve. The Itsate originally occupied a much larger region than the Apalache, covering the river valleys of extreme western North Carolina, northern Georgia and eastern Tennessee.

In contrast, the territory of Apalache Confederacy was originally enormous. This can be seen in Image 12 [**page 51**]. The southern boundary was probably near Baxley in southern Georgia. The northern boundary was near Wytheville, VA. Its territory was rather narrow in the northern section so the western boundary would have been somewhere near Rome, GA and the eastern boundary near Toccoa, GA. Farther south, the western boundary was near Auburn, AL.

Until the 1700s the Creeks' population center was roughly where Atlanta, GA is today. During the early 1700s, stark demographic shifts were caused by the impact of English and French colonization efforts. The direct descendants of the true Apalache people are the Apalachicola. Apalachicola literally means Apalache People in their Creek dialect. Today, the Apalachicola are a division of the Creek Indians. They are also known as Lower Creeks.

In their own language, they called themselves the *Apalasi,* pronounced Ă : pă : lă : shē . The word means "Light – children of." An *apala* formerly meant a torch or "source of light" in Itsate Creek, but now means a flashlight or some other source of illumination. The name may refer to the sun, which, according to Rochefort, the Apalache worshiped, but may also be a vestige of the "Time of the Sun Lords," when *hene ahau* (sun lords) came across the Gulf of Mexico to bring civilization to their ancestors. The image of rank of an Itza Maya *hene ahau* was a symbolic torch with quetzal feather flames.

The 16th century Spanish explorers were lured into the Southeast's interior by legends of "Cities of Gold" told them by Natives on the coast of Florida. Contemporary history books and Wikipedia tell us that the story was obviously an unfounded myth. Well, guess what, the stories were true . . . at least in northern Georgia and western North Carolina.

One of the many surprises found in *"Histoire naturelle et morale des îles Antilles de l'Amerique"* by Charles de Rochefort was that golden colored mica was commonly used as a decorative treatment to the stucco of public buildings in northern Georgia and western North Carolina. [2] The admixture made the buildings glisten like real gold. THAT is what started the legend of the Seven Cities of Gold.

One 17th century French explorer actually carried a bag of the mica home with him, thinking it was gold dust. The mica vaporized in the metallurgist's crucible. The traditional culture of the Creek Indians was far more similar to Mesoamerica than what Southeastern anthropologists have generally thought. However, much of the evidence has been forgotten or covered up over time.

Early Explorers and Cartographers

Juan Ponce de Leon: In 1521, Juan Ponce de Leon, died on his third voyage to Florida, where he was searching for cities of gold that were said to be somewhere in the interior.[3] He never found those cities and his surviving archives do not mention the word *Apalache*.

Álvar Cabeza de Vaca: The word *Apalache* first entered the archives of European nations in 1537. In 1527 members of the colonizing expedition of Spanish Conquistador Pánfilo de Narváez were told by Natives living near Tampa Bay that many days walking to the north were the Apalache People, who lived in large towns and had much gold. In 1536, Álvar Cabeza de Vaca was one of only four survivors of a shipwreck who made it to the coast of Mexico. The next year he wrote *La Relación*, an account of his travels. Cabeza not only retold the story of the Kingdom of Apalache, but added the statement which he constantly heard along the Gulf Coast that its cities were built of gold.

Hernando de Soto: Two years later, Hernando de Soto embarked on a better planned expedition to colonize Florida. His expedition also landed in Tampa Bay, but then marched north into what is now north central Florida. Upon entering what is now called the Tallahassee Hills Region, de Soto's men encountered a culture much more advanced that what the Spanish had seen elsewhere in the Florida Peninsula. They set up their winter encampment at the village of Anhaica Apalache. De Soto presumed that he was in the fabled Kingdom of Apalache mentioned by de Vaca.[5] From that day forward, the indigenous people of that part of Florida were called the Apalachee. Anhaica Apalache was subject to the town of Palache. Palache is the Creek name for the Biloxi Indians. The Biloxi's name for themselves was pretty close to that.

There is a catch to this famous story. As the Spaniards were leaving the "Apalachee" Province in February of 1540, they asked the locals where there was gold.[6] The Spaniards were told that if they marched northward for two weeks, they would come to the Province of Apalache. Its capital of Yupaha had much gold. It was ruled by a woman. There is something else... Depending on the dialect of the Itsate Creek language family, *Anhaica* can be translated as "metamorphosed" or "married." In modern terminology, the Apalachee in Florida were allies of the Apalache in the mountains.

De Soto headed northward in search of Yupaha until reaching a province that the Muskogeans called *Amana*. Here, he was persuaded to turn eastward to seek out a town named *Kofitachiki*. As you will learn later in this book, the Spaniards were being tricked into traveling to the arch-enemy of Apalache. Once in Kofitachiki, the Spaniards were encouraged to dig up the remains of recently deceased plague victims to retrieve their pearls. It apparently didn't dawn on the Spanish that these bodies had to be former enemies of their hosts or else carriers of some horrific plague.

A common phrase among Native peoples during that era must have been, *"Mention gold, silver, precious stones or pearls to the Spaniards and they will follow you anywhere."* The Spaniards were then guided to follow an arc around the mountain province of Apalache in order to reach Kusa, another enemy of Apalache. The de Soto Chronicles never mention the words *Yupaha* or *Apalache* after leaving the Florida Peninsula.

Diego Gutiérrez: In 1562 Diego Gutiérrez, a Spanish cartographer from the map-making studio of Casa de la Contratación, and Hieronymus Cock, a highly respected engraver living in Antwerp, collaborated in the preparation of a map of the Americas.[7] It did not mention any of the towns visited by Hernando de Soto, but did show the Province of Apalachen in the Southern Appalachian Mountains and also the Chattahoochee River flowing from this province to the Gulf of Mexico. [Image 4, page 43] Obviously, somebody after de Soto explored the interior of the Southeast from a starting point at the mouth of the Chattahoochee-Apalachicola River in the Gulf of Mexico. Their names have been lost to history.

René de Laudonnière: Also, in 1562, Captain Jean Ribault established a short-lived French colony in the southern tip of South Carolina called Charlesfort. His second-in-command was René de Laudonnière. De Laudonnière's memoir states that he stayed at Charlesfort for about a month to supervise construction of the fort, then returned to France.[8] In 1564 Captain René de Laudonnière commanded the construction of a large fort at the mouth of what all French, Spanish and English maps say was the Altamaha River.

De Laudonnière died in 1574, but the French and English versions of de Laudonniére's memoir were not published until 1586. De Laudonnièrc discussed the Kingdom of Apalache extensively. It is described as a "super-kingdom" that had political influence over many provinces because of the wealth gained from the trade of greenstone, mica, gold, silver and copper to coastal regions. The boundaries of the kingdom were two days march from the head of navigation of the Oconee River, where de Laudonnière planned to build the capital of New France. He planned to visit Apalache in October of 1565, but the massacre of Fort Caroline ended those plans. He claimed that he named the Appalachian Mountains in 1564 after an exploration party returned from there with glowing reports of the Apalache People.

Between the fall of 1564 and late summer of 1565, De Laudonnière dispatched at least six delegations to establish trade relations with Native American tribes in the interior of

Florida *Françoise*. Several of these men were away from Fort Caroline when it was massacred on September 21, 1565. The only name among these men that de Laudonnière later mentioned in his memoir was that of Pierre Gambiè. Gambiè became a trader along the Altamaha River, and he married the daughter of a provincial king. Eventually, he became king of that province.

All French maps published between 1570 and 1684 claimed the Appalachian Mountains for France. Most maps called them the "gold-bearing mountains," and contained notes which stated that René de Laudonnière had discovered and named them in 1562 while he was at Charlesfort. This statement conflicts with de Laudonnière's own memoir. However, since the 1562 Gutiérrez Map [**Image 4, page 43**] shows the Appalachian Mountains in the right location, somebody went there in 1562 or earlier.

Juan Pardo: During the summer and fall of 1567, Juan Pardo explored the southern Appalachians. His goal was to make contact with the fabled capital of Kusa that was visited in the summer of 1540 by Hernando de Soto. [9] Pardo only got as far as the capital of Chiaha, located on an island in the Little Tennessee River in a valley created by the Cheoah and Great Smoky Mountains. Pardo planned to march directly to Kusa on a route that is now U. S. 129 and GA Hwy. 52. This trail would have put him in the heart of the Province of Apalache, actually going through Track Rock Gap and the Nottely River Valley. However, Pardo received word that a large army composed of soldiers from several allied Native provinces were waiting for him in order to ambush the 30+ soldiers in his company. Pardo cancelled his plans and headed straight back to Santa Elena, which was on the coast of South Carolina, where Charlesfort had been built. The report on the Juan Pardo Expedition does not mention the word *Apalache*.

Dominique de Gourgues: Between summer of 1567 and spring of 1568, Captain Dominique De Gourgues personally financed an expedition to punish the Spanish for massacring the colonists at Fort Caroline.[10] De Gourgues met with leaders of Tacatacuru on the Medway River, about 21 miles south of present day Savannah, GA. De Gourges then disappeared into the interior of the Southeast until April 1568, where he met with his Native allies before attacking the Spanish at Fort San Mateo. This fort had been built on the ruins of Fort Caroline.

All of the forts and garrisons established by Juan Pardo in the interior of the Southeast disappeared during the exact period that Dominique de Gourgues was incognito. A combined French-Native American army massacred Fort San Mateo and two smaller forts nearby in late April of 1568. There is something else curious. For a period of almost a century after the de Gourgues Expedition, French maps alone contained detailed descriptions of the Savannah River and its tributaries. Early 18th century French maps left the Savannah River out entirely until the Colony of Georgia was settled.

Richard Hakluyt: In 1586, while he was an ambassador in Paris, Elizabethan scholar, geographer and Protestant minister, Richard Hakluyt published, *Notable Historie Containing Foure Voyages Made by Certayne French Captaynes unto Florida*.[11] This book contained the first complete saga of the efforts of the French Huguenots to colonize the South Atlantic Coast, and also introduced the knowledge of Apalache to the English public. At this time, a group of Englishmen that included Hakluyt were trying to establish a colony on Roanoke Island, North Carolina.

In 1589 Hakluyt published his landmark multi-volume book, *The Principall Navigations Voiages and Discoveries of the English Nation*, which included depositions of two former residents of Santa Catalina, who traded with the Apalache in the mountains. The Spanish called the great town on the side of a high mountain *Copal*. Copal is an aromatic resin that the Mayas burned in their temples. Charles de Rochefort stated that the priests of Apalache did not shed blood on their altars, but burned an aromatic resin constantly. This is significant evidence that the two cultures are the same.

Relación de Pedro Morales: Sir Francis Drake captured Pedro Morales when he sacked St. Augustine in 1587.[12] Morales had previously lived in Santa Elena and participated in trading expeditions to the Appalachian Mountains. Richard Hakuyt obtained a sworn deposition from Morales, which contained some valuable historical evidence, long overlooked by scholars.

Morales began by stating that there were gold and crystal mines in the Apalache Mountains. The nearest range of these mountains was 60 Spanish leagues (168 miles) northwest of Santa Elena. This would actually be the distance to Elberton, GA - about 40 miles from the Blue Ridge Mountains. It is very clear that the Cherokee Indians were not living in the Southern Highlands in the 1560s. Morales did not mention any tribe other than the Apalache. Hakluyt quoted the deposition of Morales:

"There is a great Citie, sixteene or twentie dayes journey from Santa Helena, Northwestward, which the Spaniards call La Grand Copal, which they thinke to bee very rich and exceedinglie great, and have been within sighte of it, some of them. They have offered in general to the King to take no wages of all of him, if he will leave to discover this citie, and the rich mountaines around it.

He saith also that he have seen a diamonde which was brought from the mountaines that lye west up from S. Helena. These hils seem wholy to be the mountaines of Apalatci, whereof the Savages advertised of Laudonniere, and it may bee they are the hils of Chaunis Temoatam, of which Master Lane had adverstisement of."

Relation de Nicholas Burgiognon: De Burgiongnon was one of few male occupants of Fort Caroline who was spared. [13] He apparently was a musician in his teens when Fort Caroline was attacked. Sir Francis Drake recorded

APALACHE INDIANS PANNING FOR GOLD IN A STREAM NEAR PRESENT DAY DAHLONEGA, GEORGIA

Engraving by
Theodor De Bry
1528-1598

that Burgiongnon joyfully played a Huguenot march song with his flute as he crossed the Matanzas River to be rescued by the English Protestants. Richard Hakuyt also obtained a deposition from Burgiognon. It contains considerably more information about Spanish trading activities in the mountains. It is very clear from this deposition that many Spaniards traveled to the Georgia and Carolina Mountains. The statement "taking leave at their own costs" means that they were not being chartered by the Spanish Crown. There are no records in the Spanish archives about these journeys.

At the end, Burgiognon explained that Spanish officials did not want France and England to know that Spain was exploring and prospecting the Apalache gold fields. Once Great Britain gained control of the eastern half of North America, its leaders were apparently more than happy to completely erase the knowledge that Spain had been exploring, mining and settling the Southern Highlands for 200 years prior to the arrival of the English.

Hakluyt wrote: *"He further affirmith that there is a citie Northwestward from Santa Helena in the mountains, which the Spaniards call La Grand Copal, and that in these mountaines there are great store of Christalls, Golde, Rubies and Diamondes : And that a Spaniard brought forth from thence a Diamonde which was worth 5,000 crownes. Pedro Melendes, the marques nephew to old Pedro Melendes that slew Ribault & is now governour of Florida, wear it. He saith also, that to make passage into these mountaines, it is necessary to have a store of Hatchets to give unto the Indians, and a store of Pickaxes to break the mountaines, Which shine so bright in the day in some places, that thy cannot behold them, and therefore they travel unto them by night. Also gortletz of cotton, which Spaniards call Zacopitz, are necessary to bee had, against the arrows of the Savages."*

"He saith further that a tone of the sassafras of Florida is solde in Spain for sixtie ducats : and that they have such great store of Turkie cocks, of Beanes, of Pease, and there aqre great store of Pearlses. The things, as he reportith, that the Floridians make most account of, are red Cloth, or redde Cotton to make bandraks or girdles: copper and Hatchets."

"The Spaniards have demaunded leave at their own costs, to discover the mountains, which the King of Spain denyth, for feare let the English or French would enter into the same action, once known. All the Spaniards would passe up by the river of Saint Helena unto the mountaines of Golde and Chrystall. The Spaniards entering 50 leagues from Saint Helena found Indians wearing Golde rings in their nostrils and eares. They also found Oxen, but lesse than ours. "

Theodor de Bry & Jacques Le Moyne: In 1590, Walloon engraver, Theodor de Bry, published a color map of La Florida (Southeastern United States) based on the watercolor map of Fort Caroline resident Jacques Le Moyne.[14] The map showed the Okefenokee to be a shallow lake named *Serape.* There was another shallow lake of slightly smaller size near the Altamaha River (May River) in central Georgia. This lake is where the Little Ocmulgee River Swamp is now. The town of Apalache was spelled *Apalatsi,* which is closer to its actual Creek Indian spelling. The Appalachian Mountains were shown to be approximately where northern Georgia and western North Carolina are located. [**Image 6, page 45**] *De Bry was a Walloon Protestant, just like Charles de Rochefort.*

Jodicus Hondius: Dutch cartographer, Jodicus Hondius, helped establish Amsterdam as the map-making center of the world.[15] In 1606, he published a map of Virginia and Florida, [**Image 7, page 46**] which displayed the Altamaha (May) River and the many Native towns mentioned by René de Laudonnière. He greatly enlarged the lake in central Georgia and shrunk the Okefenokee Swamp (Lake Serape.) On his maps were notes in Latin (surrounded by elaborately rendered mountains), which stated that gold and silver had been found in the Appalachian Mountains. He included a three dimensional lake in the mountains that included a note stating that Indians had obtained gold from the sands in this lake. Subsequent maps by other cartographers in the 17th century would place the supersized lake at the foot of the mountains and eliminate Lake Serape.

Willem Janszoon Bleau: Bleau was considered the leading

cartographer of his time. [16] In 1635 he published as part of a world atlas, the map, *Americae nova Tabula*. His map eliminated both large, shallow lakes on the Altamaha River, and placed the province of Apalache beyond the mountains.

Settlement of Holston River Valley: Late Colonial Era maps state that English settlement of the Holston River Valley in southwestern Virginia and northeastern Tennessee began no later than 1650. These settlers found existing towns occupied by Spanish/Portuguese speaking Jews and (separately), African Muslims. The Spanish government in Florida established a trading post and evidently a mission station on the headwaters of the Chattahoochee River in northeast Georgia during 1645.

Migration Legend of the Kussitaw People: In 1735 a delegation of the leaders of the Creek Confederacy traveled to Savannah to greet Governor James Edward Oglethorpe. [17] As a symbol of their friendship with the colonists of Georgia and Great Britain, the Tuskamiko, or Commanding General of the Palache, Chikoli, presented Oglethorpe with a bison vellum, which in the Creek writing system described the journey of the Kussitaw branch of the Creeks to Georgia. It was a true writing system rendered in black and red characters, not pictures. The vellum was translated into English. Both the vellum and its translation were immediately shipped to London, to be protected by the Archbishop of Canterbury. *The Kussitaw were listed by Charles de Rochefort in 1658 as one of the provinces of Apalache.*

The English translation of the vellum was then translated into German. By the 1820s both the original vellum and the English translation had been misplaced in the Church of England's archives. The German version was then translated back into English. That version is what is available today. Undoubtedly, there were some alterations of the original Creek proper nouns. Also, Cusseta and the Muskogee Creek used in 1735, were different dialects than was spoken by the Apalache a century earlier.

Several things are significant about the vellum. The Kusitaw sacked a great town near a temple complex on the side of Georgia's highest mountain. The temple complex was probably the Track Rock Terrace Complex. The three-way translated name of the town was Motterel. That is somewhat similar to the name of the capital town named by De Rochefort, Melilot. At that time, Palache lived in the Georgia Mountains, south of the valley where the great mountainside capital was located.

This story confirms the presence of Palache (or Apalache) in the Georgia Mountains. Secondly, the Creek general was from the town of Chikoli on the Savannah River, upstream from Savannah. That town's name appears on the map of Florida François by Jacques Le Moyne. It is confirmation that René de Laudonnière's description of towns and the Apalache being in the Georgia Mountains is trustworthy, since Chikoli was at least 120 miles from Fort Caroline.

The Reverend Charles de Rochefort

(1605-1683)

In 1651, a Walloon Protestant minister published the first edition of his book, *"Histoire naturelle et morale des îles Antilles de l'Amerique."* [18] There was no author listed on the cover, but the dedication was attributed to Philippe de Longvilliers de Poincy, Governor General of the French West Indies. The reason that he kept his name hidden was that France was going through another period of religious repression. Books by heretics (Protestants) were banned. The King of France issued a law that all books must be inspected and approved by the Holy Office (Inquisition.) Anyone selling unauthorized books would go to prison.

The first edition did not contain a description of the Kingdom of Apalache, as it predated the Brigstock Expedition to Apalache.[19] That chapter was added in the 1658 edition, this time published in Nederlander. Rochefort used his real name from then on. Versions of the book were published in French, Nederlander, English and German until 1715.

Rochefort's book is structured in two parts, the first dealing with the geographical features, and the second with the people of the Caribbean. The islands covered are listed and briefly described in chapters 3-5 of Book I.

Until recently, little was known about Rochefort. His two books continue to be of considerable interest to Dutch and French scholars because of the comprehensiveness of his descriptions of Tobago and Martinique. [20] The Gementarchief in Rotterdam preserves the "Actes des Synodes des Eglises Wallonnes," which contains manuscript notes of Charles De Rochefort about himself, the Antilles and their Protestant settlers. The man definitely existed.

De Rochefort was delegated by the Huguenot community of La Rochelle, France, to take care of the French speaking Protestant settlers scattered in the Caribbean. [21] His first stay was in La Tortuga Island, offshore present Haiti, where he acted as assistant minister or chaplain for the French Protestant Governor Le Vasseur installed there with a commission of Governor General De Poincy dated 1640. He moved to Dutch Saint-Eustachus as minister and, possibly, afterward to Tobago then ruled by the Dutch Lampsins brothers.

Returning to Europe in 1650, De Rochefort stayed in Flushing and later in Rotterdam. In Rotterdam, he became the minister of the French language Protestant church there. He continued to live in Rotterdam until 1683, when he died.

French researchers Debien and Châtillon think that, once back to Holland in 1650, De Rochefort used a relationship he had made with the actual French Protestant Minister in Tobago, Reverend Du Chillou. [22] Rochefort copied documents loaned to him by the Lampsins brothers . Both

CHARLES DE ROCHEFORT

1605-1683

of these Dutch merchants had been made baronnets of Tobago by French King Louis the 14th. Debien, Chatillon and Boucher are sure that De Rochefort was paid by the Lampsin Brothers for his writings. The scholars think that they also paid for the printing of the book on Tobago.[23] It is quite possible that the Brigstock Family of Barbados paid Rochefort to include the chapter on Apalache.

No matter when or where he was traveling in the Caribbean Basin, De Rochefort is, himself, proof of the Walloon Protestant presence in Caribbean Islands, and the link between the French Huguenots and the Dutch merchants, many or most of whom were Sephardic Jews. The key role of both maritime cities of La Rochelle and Flushing is also ascertained by statements made in his books. The date and place of his death are not known.

The Chapter on the Kingdom of Apalache

Rochefort was particularly interested in indigenous peoples and languages. The book includes a detailed chapter on the Kingdom of Apalache in the Georgia Mountains, as well as a vocabulary of the Caraïbe language prepared by Raymond Breton (1609-79), a Jesuit priest sent by Cardinal Richelieu (with Du Terte) to Guadeloupe in the 1630s. [23] The chapter on Apalache is attributed to the statements of a Mr. Brigstock, who arrived in the Kingdom of Apalache in 1653.

Apalache was the name of the original Creek Indian Confederacy. The chapter on the Kingdom of Apalache contains the most detailed description of Creek Indian history, politics, architecture, clothing and religion prior to assimilation of European culture, produced in the Colonial Period. These accounts of Native Americans in the Southeast derived from Mr. Brigstock's writings about his extensive tour of Apalache.

Rochefort was the minister for French-speaking Protestants in the Caribbean, but apparently he also worked with

English Protestants. According to the Library of Congress the portion of the book about the Caribbean islands is based on Rochefort's personal observations and the writings of previous authors, notably the Dominican priest Jean-Baptiste Du Terte (1610-87). [25] Members of Protestant congregations on various islands also contributed detailed geographical information.

In 1666 the book was translated by John Davies into English and printed by T. Dring and J. Starkey in London, England. It was named, "*The History of the Caribby-Islands.*"[26] Later printings of the book were published in Rochefort's name, and included several lithographs created by Rotterdam engraver, Chez Arnout Leers. The most elaborate of these lithographs portrays the capital of Apalache in the Georgia Mountains. It was engraved in 1665 and entitled, "*Paysage de la Province de Bemarin au Royaume d'Apalache.*"

Mr. Brigstock: Many contemporary scholars have assumed that the "Mr. Brigstock," (the man who supposedly toured the Province of Apalache) was a fictional character in whose mouth, Rochefort put descriptions of a fantasy world that never existed. This is highly unlikely. The Brigstock family was prominent in Barbados. The name was spelled various ways, including "Briggstock" and "Briggstocke." In 1659 several Brigstocks moved from Barbados and joined the Virginia aristocracy. Had Rochefort put false words into Mr. Brigstock's mouth, he would have been brought to trial and probably jailed. Slander and falsifying statements were felonies back then. At the time that Mr. Brigstock was touring the Southern Highlands, there was chaos in Barbados. Its assembly had declared independence from Great Britain. There was a real reason for Brigstock to be away from home.

Richard Brigstock witnessed the following documents in March and August of 1649: [27]

Briggstock, Richard , planter

Christ Church Parish, 15 Nov 1684

Sons William Briggstock & John Briggstock—land under the Rock that joins land of George Ocher, John Maccomary, & John Jones; son Richd: Briggstock ; dau Mary; wf Mary Bristocke; Xtrs—Lithard Parsons & John Gaage (original book names Richard Carsonne & John Gragge). signed Richard (x) Briggstock

Wit: John (x) Gragge, Richard Parsons, John (x) OMahony, William Harbort (original book names John Gagge, Richard Carsonne, John Mattony, William Harbort)

Proved 26 Feb 1685

Christ Church records show that his son Richard Briggstock and his wife Mary had a daughter Mary on 18 Jan 1665, and a son, William, 24 Feb 1666.

The Book's Reception

Rochefort's book was considered factual and an excellent resource by scholars and cartographers in late 17th century England, France and the Netherlands. Other publications continued to obtain more information on the Apalache. [28] For example, an English book published in 1671, *America, Being the Latest, and Most Accurate Description of the New World,* contained the following information:

"Amongst others, the Apalachites make mention in their Areitos, or songs, of a king called Maydo, eminent for his noble achievements, and prudent governing of his people." Today, *mvto* (pronounced Maydo) is the Creek word for "thank you."

Nicholas Sanson: In 1650, cartographer Nicholas Sanson, included the capital of Apalache, Melilot, on his map, *"Amerique Septentrionale."*[29] **[Image 8, page 47]** The name *Apalache* or both Apalache and Melilot appeared French maps until 1717. The maps also included, just as Rochefort wrote, the Kusa Indians being in NW Georgia and branches of the Creek Indians living in western North Carolina and eastern Tennessee.

Robert Mordon: Most of the 17th century maps inaccurately placed the source of the May (Altamaha) River inside the mountains of Apalache. De Laudonnière did not say this. He said that the May River began in the foothills of the mountains. In 1693 English cartographer, Robert Morden, accurately placed the capital of Apalache at the headwaters of the Chattahoochee River. [30] This was the last British map to show the Apalache Province in northern Georgia. [**Image 8, page 47**]

Bernard Picart and Jean Frederic Bernard: Typical of the dozens of books that mentioned Apalache until the mid-1700s was, *"The Religious Ceremonies and Customs of the Several Nations of the Known World."* It was published in 1731 by Bernard Picart and Jean Frederic Bernard. [31]

"The inhabitants of Apalache embalm the bodies of their relations and deceased friends, and leave them almost three months in the balm; they are afterwards dry'd with aromatic drugs, wrapp'd up in rich furs, and laid in cedar coffins, which the relations keep for twelve moons at their own houses: then they carry it to neighboring forest, and bury it at the foot of a tree. But they shew a greater regard for the bodies of their Paraoustis; for they first embalm them, then dress them up with all their ornaments, set 'em off with feathers and necklaces, and afterwards keep 'em for three years together in the apartment where they died, all which time they lie in those wooden coffins above-mentioned; at the expiration of which, they are deposited in the sepulchres of their predecessors up on the side of the mountain of Olaimy."

"They are let down into a cave, the mouth of which they

stop with great flint-stones, hanging on the branches of the neighboring trees the weapons they made use of in war, as so many testimonies of their bravery. 'Tis further said, that the nearest relations plant a cedar near the cave, which they dress with care in honor of the deceased. Whenever the tree dies, they immediately plant another in its place."

"The Apalachites believe in the immortality of the soul, and that those who have liv'd a life of virtue are carried up into heaven and lodg'd among the stars; but they fix the habitation of the wicked in the precipices of the high mountains of the north, among the bears, and in the midst of ice and snow."

French and British Competition

English appreciation of the book began to chill in the 1670s as France and Great Britain began to compete head on for control of North America. After 1669, no British map showed the occupants of the Georgia Mountains and extreme southeastern Tennessee until the end of the French & Indian War in 1763. The Creek and Shawnee Indians in these regions were viewed as French allies or at least, as not being confirmed British allies.

Most British scholars stopped discussing the Apalache after around 1700. There were still many entries about the Apalache in French volumes until the end of the French & Indian War.

Until 1717, French maps showed the province of Apalache controlling a small area that included the north-central Georgia Mountains and the area around Murphy, NC. This is exactly as Rochefort had described their shrunken territory in 1659. After 1717, the word Apalache is missing. [Image 11, page 50] From then until 1763, the French maps showed northern Georgia being mainly occupied by branches of the Creek Indians; the Kusa, Apalachicola and the Kowita.

The Apalachicolas were part of the same ethnic group that occupied the Mountain Apalache province, but these villages on the Etowah River had moved northward from the Chattahoochee River in 1645.

Apparently, the Mountain Apalaches were crushed by the Cherokees in the opening stages of the Creek-Cherokee War in 1717. This is not known for certain, however. Afterward, the still powerful Upper Creeks moved to occupy Apalache. The Upper Creeks and Coweta Creeks continued to occupy, or at least claim most of the old province of Apalache until 1785, when most was given to the Cherokees as their new hunting territory. The Koweta Creeks continued to occupy a narrow corridor leading northward to the eastern end of the Nacoochee Valley until 1818.

What happened to the Apalache?

The disappearance of the Apalache from European maps in the early 1700s has influenced many anthropologists, who are almost ignorant of Creek Indian history and culture, to assume that their existence was a myth. However, the Apalache's disappearance from the Georgia Mountains coincided with the construction of Fort Toulouse by the French in 1717 and the start of the Creek-Cherokee War. Something else happened just before then.

In 1715 all of the major Native American tribes rose up simultaneously and killed the South Carolina traders in their territories. The inscription, "Liube 1715" was carved on the Track Rock petroglyphs. [32] Track Rock Gap was the gateway to the sacred Valley of the Hemlocks that was Apalache "inner sanctum" and religious capital. It is now known as the Nottely River Valley. Liube is a female Jewish name meaning "Beloved," and Liube was either seeking sanctuary in this valley or being abducted away from it.

A few weeks later, all of the "Creek" leaders were invited to a diplomatic conference at the Cherokee (*actually whatever a Cherokee was back then*) town of Tugaloo. There was no such thing as a Creek Indian in 1715. Undoubtedly the leaders of Apalache were invited. They were all killed in their sleep. The Cherokees immediately grabbed a large swath of land, because they had more muskets than anyone else. A forty year long war was begun.

The disorganized provinces and principal towns of the old Kingdom of Apalache found themselves fighting both the British and the Cherokees without access to British munitions that they formerly had obtained from the British. They had no choice but to move closer to Fort Toulouse, where the French could provide them gunpowder and musket balls. Thus, in a matter of perhaps as few as two years, the population center of the Creek Indians shifted from northern Georgia to roughly Columbus, GA.

France "claimed" all of Apalache west of the Blue Ridge Mountains because its surveyors had mapped the rivers that flow into the Gulf of Mexico. The hidden hand of France was very much behind the Yamasee War (1715-1717.) In 1705 Pierre Le Moyne d'Iberville wrote the first known battle plan as a strategy for driving the British out of the Southeast. [33] Every detail of the first stage of the Yamasee War was straight out of his battle plan.

Le Moyne died around 1706 of malaria, but the printed plan stayed with French authorities. The first step was to eliminate the dependency of the Southeastern tribes on British supplies. The tribes were encouraged to kill the South Carolina traders. They didn't think about where they would be getting gunpowder once the sources of all their munitions had been murdered. Perhaps the French had promised to supply them, but France did not have the capability of supporting so many warriors at one time. The switching of sides by the Cherokees doomed the plan, because it stretched out the war beyond the logistical level that France could support.

Out of gunpowder and musket balls, many of the principal Apalache towns closest to the Cherokees fled their homeland and literally clustered around Fort Toulouse for protection. We learn this from a French book written in 1752.

Memoires sur l'Amerique et Sur l'Africa by Etienne Andre Phillipe de Pretot book proves that there was substantial truth to Rochefort's book.[34] These four divisions of the Creek Confederacy appear in early 18th century French maps as towns near Fort Toulouse at the confluence of the Coosa and Tallapoosa Rivers, but also are divisions of the Creek Confederacy today.

"*Two sorts of people live here, the Natives of the country and the Spanish. The Natives of the country make up five or six little nations, among the best known and most civilized is that of the Apalaches: They have a sovereign called Paracousse, who resides in Melilot in the region of Bemarin to the north since he abandoned the town of Apalache: the chiefs of the other nations recognize Paracousse as Sovereign; their names and their towns are Conchatez [Quasarte Tribal Town], Conchaques [Apalachicola Tribe Town], Alibamou [Alabama Tribe], Caouita [Koweta Tribal Town].*"

All Creek and Alabama towns used the title of Mako or Mekko for their chiefs. Just as the Spanish used the Caribbean word, cacique, for all Native American chiefs, apparently the French used the word, *paracousse,* for all Native American chiefs.

Reliability of Native American Words

There is no letter "B" in the Creek languages. Since the Province of Bemarin is clearly not a Muskogean word, it is strongly suspected that Bemarin was used by the French, but was not the actual name of the province. [35] The situation is comparable to English speakers calling the people of the Netherlands, Dutch, or calling the land known to its inhabitants as Sverige, Sweden.

A majority of the names that Rochefort gave for Native American provinces are highly suspect. They do not appear to be Muskogean words. They appear French in character. A minority of the provincial names DO closely resemble Muskogean names for ethnic groups or provinces. None of the personal names provided are Muskogean, but are Hebrew names. The discrepancy of the majority of proper nouns is highly significant. All of the political titles and names of towns in the Southern Highlands, recorded by the chroniclers of the de Soto and Pardo Expedition can be translated by either Creek or Maya Indian dictionaries. Mr. Brigstock may have made up many of the words, forgotten their correct pronunciation, or, perhaps, Sephardic Jews had intermarried into the elite of Apalache a generation or two before Brigstock's journey through Apalache.

Rochefort's book was largely forgotten in Great Britain after the early 1700s. France claimed most of northern Georgia and all of western North Carolina until 1763 so there was some continuing interest among French scholars in the chapter on the Apalache for a few more decades.

Rochefort wrote a second book on Tobago and Martinique. After France lost all of its possessions in North America in 1763, it still had some possessions such as Martinique and Dominica. Rochefort's books provided valuable anthropological information on these islands. However, the chapter on the Apalache People seemed like a fairy tale about an ethnic group that never existed. It was completely ignored or its information was mistakenly applied to articles on the Apalachee Indians of Florida, with a caveat attached that the geographical information was fictional.

Contemporary Scholars

Charles de Rochefort's two books continue to be of major interest to French, Dutch and Caribbean Island scholars because of their detailed information on the French, Dutch and Sephardic Jewish colonists in the 1600s. The books also discuss indigenous peoples in the Caribbean, who are now extinct. They are considered to be highly accurate descriptions of the history and culture of the Caribbean Indigenous Peoples. As recently as 2011, a French historian wrote a book on his work.

North American scholars and anthropologists have generally ignored Rochefort's books and seem to not be aware how much his work is respected in Europe. Typifying this attitude is the bin in which original copies of Rochefort's books are stored at the Carter Brown Library. It is labeled "Utopian Fantasies."

There are several reasons for the lack of respect for Rochefort's books. They all are rooted in the misunderstanding of Early Colonial History in North America and of the Creek Indians in general. *Florida* was originally the name of all of the lower section of what is now the United States. The ethnic labels *Apalache, Timucua* and *Guale* were assigned by the Spanish to indigenous peoples in northern Florida and southeastern Georgia without regard to what they called themselves. Each label was merely a name of a single village. Thus when an anthropologist reads a book about the indigenous people in the mountains of Florida, he or she immediately assumes that it is poppycock.

One of the more common criticisms of the chapter on Apalache is, "*Temples and cities built of stone on the sides of Georgia Mountains? This is obviously a fantasy!*" Charles C. Jones, the first archaeologist in Georgia stated that there were many stone ruins in the northern half of Georgia when the first English colonists arrived. Most of them were quickly converted into chimneys and foundation walls. Those in remote locations such as mountain tops were often converted into crushed stone for highway construction. For example, there was once a complex ellipse-shaped stone observatory on top of Ladds Mountain near Etowah Mounds (Cartersville, GA.) In the late 1930s it became the crushed stone base for the first paved state highway between Cartersville and Dallas, GA. All that remains today are a few rocks and some grainy black & white photos.

The location that most closely matched the Rochefort's description of the Valley of Hemlocks where, the capital of Apalache was located, is now called the Nottely River Valley. It is in Union County, GA, immediately west of Georgia's highest mountain, Brasstown Bald. Within that valley are at least a dozen stone, Native American-built ruins. The largest of these is the Track Rock Terrace Complex that covers a half square mile. The immensely popular premier of the History Channel's "America Unearthed" was about the Track Rock site.

Other readers are confused by the book's statements, which placed an advanced Muskogean people throughout the mountains of Georgia and western North Carolina in 1653. The book does not mention the Cherokee Indians or a word similar to Cherokee. The only other indigenous people that Rochefort discussed was an aggressive tribe associated with the Caribbean Islands that temporarily invaded the mountains and occupied some valleys. Some of these "Caribbeans" still remained at the time the book was written. De Rochefort's description of the indigenous inhabitants conflicts with the Cherokees' claim to have been the sole occupants of the region for 10,000 years.

Once the reader gets past the questionable ethnic names, there are many details in the book that have the ring of authenticity. In particular, De Rochefort's description of the architecture is very specific and can be collaborated. Many of the details he described in the architecture were not known by archaeologists until the late 20th century.

The History of the Caribby-Islands probably contains some errors caused by the European observers not being fluent in the indigenous language. It is quite possible that the meanings of some words were lost in translation from one tongue to another. As far as Mr. Brigstock is concerned, there is a strong possibility that he originally heard about the Province of Apalache from Dutch Jewish traders, who had earlier visited the area. Overall, it is by far the most detailed description available for the Creek Indians in the mid-1600s. Without this book, much of the 1600s would be a "black hole" for historians, who are studying the Southern Highlands.

References and Notes

1. The territory of the Apalache generally conforms to the boundaries of the region where indigenous peoples were known to speak one of the Creek languages in 1540, when Hernando de Soto passed through the region.

2. De Rochefort, Charles, **The History of the Caribby-Islands,** (1666 in English).

3. Davis, T. Frederick. (1935) "History of Juan Ponce de Leon's Voyages to Florida: Source Records." Florida Historical Society Quarterly. V14:1.

4. Cabeza de Vaca, Álvar Núñez, **The Narrative of Cabeza De Vaca, Translation of La Relación**, Rolena Adorno and Patrick Charles Pautz. Lincoln, NE: University of Nebraska Press 2003.

5. **The De Soto Chronicles,** Account by the Gentleman of Elvas, Chapter XII , p. 71-72.

6. Ibid. p. 74.

7. "A Modern and Quite Precise Depiction of America (or the Fourth Part of the World)" .World Digital Library.

8. De Laudonnière, René, **L'histoire notable de la Floride, contenant les trois voyages faits en icelles par des capitaines et pilotes français**, 1586.

9. De la Bandera, Juan, **Relación de Florida** (Juan Pardo Expedition), 1569.

10. Hakluyt, Richard, **The Principall Navigations Voiages and Discoveries of the English Nation** (Imprinted at London, 1589) Introduction.

11. Hakluyt, Richard, **The Principall Navigations Voiages and Discoveries of the English Nation** (Imprinted at London, 1589) Volume 9, "The Fourth French Voiage."

12. Ibid., **Relación de Pedro Morales**

13. Ibid., **Relación de Nicholas Burgiognon**

14. Harriot, Thomas, **A briefe and true Report of the new found Land**

of Virginia. The complete 1590 edition with 28 engravings by Theodor de Bry, after the drawings of John White and other illustrations. British Museum. Dover Publications, Inc. (1972); pp. 91.

15. Peter van der Krogt (ed.): **Koeman's atlantes Neerlandici,** Vol. 1: *The folio atlases published by Gerard Mercator, Jodocus Hondius, Henricus Hondius, Johannes Janssonius and their successors,* 't Goy-Houten 1997.

16. Krogt, van der, Peter CJ(2000), **Koeman's Atlantes Neerlandici** Vol. II: *The Folio Atlases Published by Willem Jansz. Blaeu and Joan Blaeu,* Houten: Hes & De Graaf publishers BV

17. Gatschlet, Albert S., **The Migration Legend of the Creek People,** Philadelphia: D. C. Blanton, 1884, pp. 249-251.

18. De Rochefort, Charles, **The History of the Caribby-Islands,** (1666 in English) Chapter VIII – "By way of Digression giving an account of the Apalachites, the Nature of their Country, their Manners, and their ancient and modern Religion."

19. Roux, Benoit, *"Le pasteur Charles De Rochefort et l'Histoire naturelle et morale des îles Antilles de l'Amérique,"* Ingénieur d'études (Programme ANR)/Doctorant – Université de Reims Champagne-Ardenne, 2013.

20. Huyghues-Belrose, Vincent, **Études Caribéennes,** "The early colonization of Tobago: bibliographical and archival material in Martinique and France," 2007.

21. Roux, Benoit, Ibid.

22. Chatillon, Marcel & Debien, Gabriel. 1981. "La propagande imprimée pour les Antilles et la Guyane au XVIIe siècle, recrutement ou racolage ?", Annales des Antilles, n° 24, 1981, pp. 57-98. p. 84-88 : Vers Tobago avec le ministre Rochefort. Analysis of the book published during the Dutch dominion of Tobago by Charles De Rochefort.

23. Rochefort, Charles de. 1665. Le tableau de l'Isle de Tobaggo, ou de la Nouvelle Oüalchre, L'une des isles Antilles de l'Amérique, Leyde, 1665, Paris, 1667, avec enrichissements du pasteur Du Chillou.

24. De Rochefort, Charles, **The History of the Caribby-Islands,** Ibid.

25. Library of Congress, "Charles de Rochefort."

26. Roux, Benoit, Ibid.

27. Archives of Christ Church Parish, Barbados.

28. Ogilby, John, **America: Being the Latest, and Most Accurate Description of the New World**, London:1671, p.354.

29. Sanson, Nicholas, "Amerique Septentrionale," 1669.

30. Morden, Robert, **A New Map of the English Empire in America**, viz Virginia, Maryland, Carolina, Pennsylvania, New York, New Iarsey, New England, Newfoundland, New France &c by Rob Morden . . . Sold by Robt. Morden at the Atlas in Cornhill. And by Christopher Brown at ye Globe near the Westend of St. Pauls; London, 1565.

31. Picart, Bernard & Benard, Jean Frederic, **The Religious Ceremonies and Customs of the Several Nations of the Known World**, 1731, (Vol. III - page 121).

32. Thornton, Richard, "Stone inscription proves early presence of Jewish settlers in the Appalachians," The Examiner, April 11, 2011.

33. Crouse, Nellis Maynard, **Lemoyne d'Iberville: Soldier of New France**. Ithaca: Cornell University Press, 1954.

34. De Pretot, Etienne Andre, "Memoires sur l'Amerique et Sur l'Africa"

35. Richard Thornton is a "card carrying" Creek Indian.

MAPS

1562 Map of the Americas by
Diego Gutiérrez & Hieronymus Cock

Gutiérrez put the lands discovered by Hernando de Soto in
Texas and labeled the region 'The Land of the Chichimecs."

Chattahoochee River

Apalachen   **Savannah River**

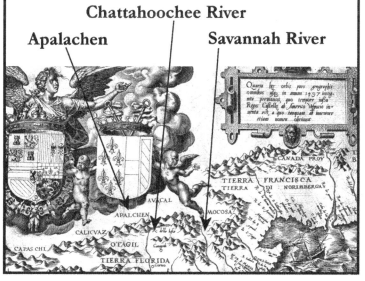

IMAGE 4

1578 Map of La Florida by Diego Gutiérrez

In this update of his 1562 map, Gutiérrez clearly showed
the May River to be one and the same as the Altamaha River.
He drew a fairly accurate path for the Rio de Spiritu Santos
(Chattahoochee) and placed Apalache at its headwaters.

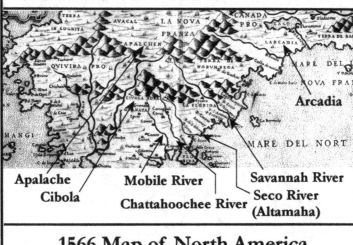

Apalache
Cibola

Mobile River

Chattahoochee River

Arcadia

Savannah River
Seco River
(Altamaha)

1566 Map of North America
by Paolo Forlani

IMAGE 5

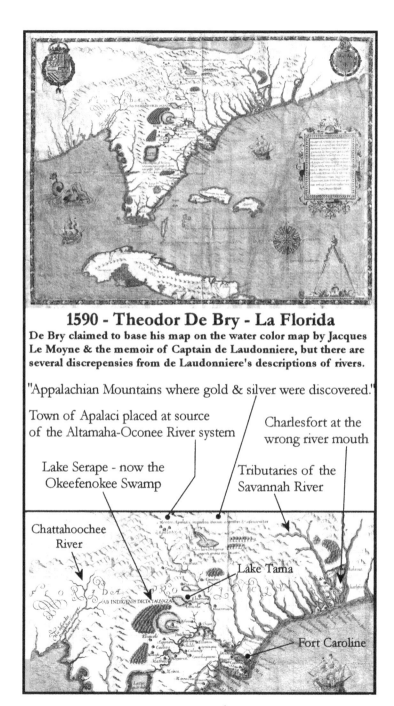

1590 - Theodor De Bry - La Florida

De Bry claimed to base his map on the water color map by Jacques Le Moyne & the memoir of Captain de Laudonniere, but there are several discrepensies from de Laudonniere's descriptions of rivers.

"Appalachian Mountains where gold & silver were discovered."

Town of Apalaci placed at source of the Altamaha-Oconee River system

Charlesfort at the wrong river mouth

Lake Serape - now the Okeefenokee Swamp

Tributaries of the Savannah River

Chattahoochee River

Lake Tama

Fort Caroline

IMAGE 6

1606 - Jodicus Hondius

Hondius based the interior of his map on the explorations of the Fort Caroline and Roanoke Island colonies. Someone had paddled up the Savannah River because it was extremely accurate. The town of Apalache was no longer shown near the source of the Altamaha-Oconee River system. Lake Serape (Okeefenokee Swamp) was shown, but Lake Tama was grossly oversized and placed in the foothills of the Blue Ridge Mts.

Apalatcy Mountains Gold-bearing

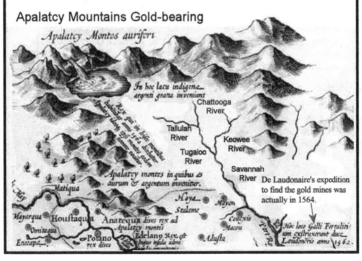

IMAGE 7

1650 - Nicholas Sanson
Detail of his map of North America

This is the earliest known official map to show the town of
Melilot and Apalache as a nation. Lake May (Tama) is grossly
out of proportion and too far inland. The Chattahoochee River
is fairly accurate. This reflects Spanish exploration. Brigstock
apparently visited Apalache in 1653 after seeing this map.

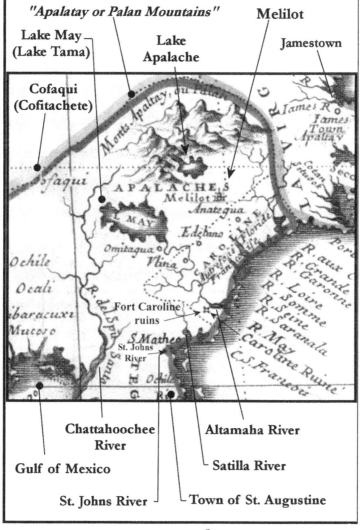

"Apalatay or Palan Mountains"   Melilot

Lake May (Lake Tama)   Lake Apalache   Jamestown

Cofaqui (Cofitachete)

Chattahoochee River   Altamaha River

Gulf of Mexico   Satilla River

St. Johns River   Town of St. Augustine

IMAGE 8

1693 - Robert Mordon

By 1693, South Carolina traders had been going out into the region for over 22 years. The town of Apalache is shown to be in the Nacoochee Valley near the Chattahoochee's source. Here a British Army party saw dozens of smoke plumes from "Spaniards" smelting gold. The town would never appear on another map. It was obviously destroyed per Britain's request.

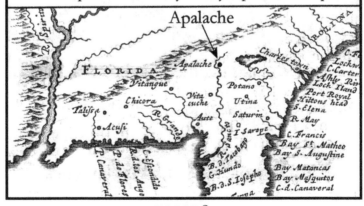

IMAGE 9

48

1703 - Guillaume Delisle

In his famous map of Lousiana & Mexico, Guillaume Delisle showed the upper Tennessee Valley to be occupied by Muskogeans, the province of Apalache still thriving in the Georgia Mountains, plus the Kusa and Conchakee's in NW Georgia. The Cofachite's (Caribs) had at some time in the previous decade occupied sections of the North Carolina Mountains. In earlier maps, they had been in north-central Tennessee. Late 17th century Virginia archives talk about a rootless tribe that ravaged the Southeast's Native landscape.

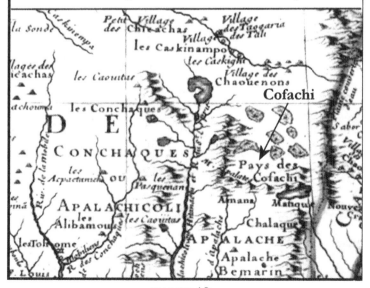

IMAGE 10

1718 - Guillaume Delisle

Delisle mapped a stark change in the Southern Highlands between 1701 and 1718. Apalache completely disappeared along with the Cofitachi. A new tribe called the Cheraqui now occupied northeastern Tennessee and the northwestern tip of South Carolina. This change coincides with the findings of archaeologist Joe Caldwell, who calculated that the ancient town of Ustanauli had been burned between 1700 and 1715 then was replaced by a small Cherokee village named Tugaloo.

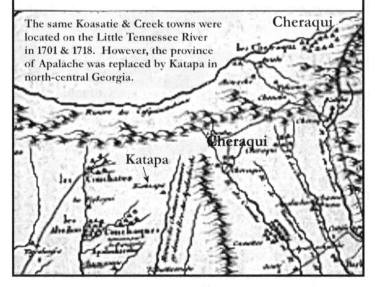

The same Koasatie & Creek towns were located on the Little Tennessee River in 1701 & 1718. However, the province of Apalache was replaced by Katapa in north-central Georgia.

IMAGE 11

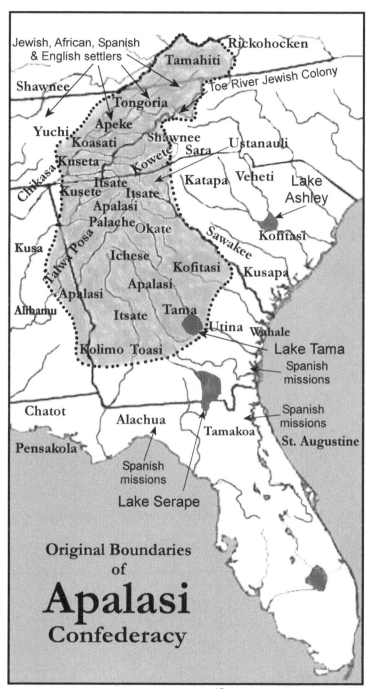

Jewish, African, Spanish & English settlers

Rickohocken

Tamahiti

Toe River Jewish Colony

Shawnee

Tongoria

Apeke

Yuchi

Koasati

Shawnee

Ustanauli

Kuseta

Kowete

Sara

Chikasa

Itsate

Katapa

Veheti

Lake Ashley

Kusete

Itsate

Apalasi

Palache

Okate

Kofitasi

Kusa

Takwa Posa

Ichese

Sawakee

Kofitasi

Kusapa

Apalasi

Apalasi

Alibamu

Itsate

Tama

Utina

Wahale

Kolimo Toasi

Lake Tama

Spanish missions

Chatot

Alachua

Spanish missions

Tamakoa

St. Augustine

Pensakola

Spanish missions

Lake Serape

Original Boundaries
of
Apalasi
Confederacy

IMAGE 12

51

Of the Origine of the Caribbians, the Natural Inhabitants of the Country

Notes by Richard Thornton will follow original passages.

MELILOT

THE CAPITAL CITY
OF THE
KINGDOM OF APALACHE

VISITED BY MR. BRIGSTOCK,
AN ENGLISHMAN,
IN 1653

In all the several sentiments whereof we have given an account, either out of the Writings or Discourses of divers others, there is this that's commendable, That those who advance them, proceed consequently to the discoveries they had made, and that they do all that lies in their power to unravel and disengage ancient and unknown Truths. But if the Relation we are about to give of the Origine of the *Caribbian* Inhabitants of the Islands, be the most ample, the most particular, the most full of Curiosities, and the best circumstanc'd of any that hath hitherto appear'd, it is but just we should think it accordingly the truest and most certain; yet with this caution, that we still leave the judicious Reader at liberty to follow that sentiment which shall seem most rational to him. And whereas we ought to render every one the commendation he justly deserves, we are to acquaint the Publick, that it is oblig'd for these Particularities and Discoveries to the obliging Communication we have receiv'd thereof from one Master *Brigstock* an *English* Gentleman, one of the most curious and inquisitive Persons in the World, who, among his other great and singular accomplishments, hath attained the perfection of the *Virginian* and *Floridian* Languages, as having in his noble Travels seen all the Islands, and a great part of Septentrional America: By that means it was that he came exactly to understand, upon the very place whereof we shall make mention, and from such intelligent Persons as could give him account thereof with some certainty, the ensuing History of the Origine of our Savages, the truth whereof he will make good whenever occasion shall require.

The *Caribbians* were originary Inhabitants of the Septentrional part of America, of that Country which is now called Florida: They came to inhabit the Islands after they had departed from amidst the *Apalachites*, among whom they lived a long time; and they left there some of their people, who to this day go under the name of *Caribbians*: But their first origine is from the *Cofachites*, who only chang'd their denomination, and were called *Caribbians* in the Country of the *Apalachites*, as we shall see anon.

Apalachite is the Anglicization of the Itsate (Hitchiti) Creek words Apala-si-te, which mean "Children of Light People. The words are pronounced Ă : pă : lă ´ shē : tē.

Prior to the arrival of Arawaks, Cuba and the Antilles were occupied by the Ciboney People. Some were still living in western Cuba when Cuba was colonized by Spain. Several anthropologists have theorized that the Ciboney originally lived in the Florida Peninsula, and colonized Cuba from there.

Charles Rochefort described another Caribbean population that also originated in Florida. Most of its population migrated to the Antilles. The residual population had good relations with the Apalache for many years.

The *Apalachites* are a powerful and generous Nation, which continues to this present planted in the same Country of *Florida*: They are the Inhabitants of a gallant and spacious Country called *Apalacha*, from which they have received their name, and which begins at the altitude of thirty three degrees and twenty five minutes, North of the Equinoctial Line, and reaches to the thirty seventh degree. This people have a communication with the Sea of the Great Gulf of *Mexico* or *New*

Spain, by the means of a River, which taking its source out of the *Apalachæan* Mountains, at the foot whereof they inhabit, after it hath wandered through many rich Campagnes, disembogues itself at last into the Sea neer the Islands of *Tacobago*: The Spaniards have called this River *Riu del Spirito Santo*; but the *Apalachites* call it still by its ancient name of *Hitanachi,* which in their Language signifies fair and pleasant. On the East-side they are divided from all other Nations by high and far-spreading Mountains, whose tops are cover'd with snow most part of the year, and which separate them from *Virginia*: on the other sides they adjoin to several inconsiderable Nations, which are all their friends and confederates.

The Rio de Espirito Santo was the Chattahoochee River. The Blue Ridge Mountains were called the Snowy Mountains in the 1500s and 1600s. Accounts from that era stated that they were snow-covered most of the winter. That is no longer the case. The nations to the west were the ancestors of the Alabama, Choctaw and Chickasaw Tribes.

The Tocobago's were a fierce tribe that occupied Tampa Bay region of Florida until the 1700s. They were enemies of both the Calusa and Timucua's.

The *Apalachites* make it their boast, that they had propogated certain Colonies a great way into *Mexico*; And they show to this day a great Road by land, by which they affirm that their Forces march'd into those parts. The Inhabitants of the Country, upon their arrival gave them the name of *Tlatuici*, which signifies *Mountaineers* or *High-Landers*, for they were more hardy and more generous than they. They planted themselves in a quarter like that from which they came, scituate at the foot of the Mountains, in a fertile soil, where they built a City, as neer as they could like that which they had left behind them, whereof they are possess'd to this day. They are so united there by inter-marriages and other bonds of peace, that they make up but one people with them; nor in deed could they be well discern'd one from the other, if they had not retain'd several words of their originary language, which is the only observable difference between them.

The original story probably was that the Apalache had established colonies on the Gulf Coast of Mexico. In the translation from Apalache to English to French and then back to English, the story was modified.

"Tlatuici" was actually the Talwa-hvlwe-se, which means "Offspring of Highland Towns" in the Creek languages. This colony was probably located in the Gulf Coast of the Florida Panhandle, Alabama or Mississippi. The real name of the Biloxi on the Gulf Coast was Palachi. The description of the colony also matches the ethnic group that the Spanish called the Apalachee in the Florida Panhandle near Tallahassee. These people called themselves the Alachua, but had two towns named *Apalache* and *Apalachien*.

After the *Apalachites* had planted this Colony, the *Cofachites*, who liv'd more towards the north of *America*, in a fenny and somewhat barren Country, and who had continu'd till then in good correspondence with them, knowing that they were then far from their best and most valiant men, took an advantageous opportunity to fall upon their Neighbours the *Apalachites*, and to force them out of their habitations, or at least to participate with them of the land where they had setled themselves, after they should become Masters thereof.

Kofachi-te means "Mixed People" in the Itsate (Hitchiti) Creek language spoken in most of Georgia. Its name in the Muskogee Creek language, Kofitachi-ke, appeared as a South Carolina indigenous town visited by de Soto in late spring of 1540.

The barren, swampy land where the Cofachites live may be the Low Country of South Carolina, where the town of Kofitachike was located. The original center of the Cofachites could have also been the ceremonial complex in Savannah, GA, known as the Irene Complex. In 1540, the province of Kofita was located in east-central Georgia, immediately west of the Savannah River.

This design having been carried on very cunningly among the chiefest of the *Cofachites*, they afterwards publish'd it in all their Villages, and got it approv'd by all the heads of Families, who instead of minding the business of Husbandry and setting things in order for the sowing of Corn at the beginning of Spring, as they were wont to do other years, prepar'd their Bows, Arrows, and Clubs; and having set their habitations on fire, and furnish'd themselves with some little provisions out of what was left of the precedent Winter, they took the field, with their wives and children, and all the little baggage they had, with a resolution to conquer or dye, since they had cut off all hopes of returning to a place which they had destroy'd and despoil'd of all manner of coveniences.

In this equipage they in a short time got to the frontiers of their Neighbors: the *Apalachites* who thought of nothing less than having an enemy so neer them, were then very busie about the planting of their *Mais*, and the roots from which they derive their ordinary sustenance: Those who lived about the great Lake at the foot of the Mountains, which they call in their Language *Theomi*, having perceiv'd this powerful

Army ready to fall on them, immediately made their retreat into the neighbouring Mountains, and left their villages and cattel to the disposal of the enemy; thence they took their march through the woods, to carry intelligence of the erruption to the Cities which are in the vallies among the first mountains, where resided the *Paracoussis*, who is the King of the Country, with all the considerable forces thereof. Upon this so unexpected news, the said Prince, while he was making his preparations to go against the Enemy, posted those who were most in a readiness for the expedition in the Avenues of the Mountains, and placed Ambuscadoes in several parts of the great Forests, which lie between the great Lake and the Mountains, and through which there was a necessity of passing to get into that pleasant and spacious valley, which is above sixty leagues in length, and about ten in breadth; where are the habitations of the chiefest Inhabitants of the Country, and the most considerables Cities in the Kingdom.

The word, Paracoussis, was the English mistranslation of the French word, *Paracousse*, in the original French text written by Charles Rochefort. Obviously, Rochefort had read the memoir of Captain René de Laudonnière, commander of Fort Caroline between 1564 and 1565. Several of the provinces on the coast of Georgia and South Carolina were of South American ancestry. They used the Peruvian title of Paracus for their high kings. The Paracus people built the famous Nazca Lines in Peru during the period between 450 AD and 600 AD.

Rochefort assumed that the Apalache (Muskogean) peoples in the interior of the Southeast also used this title. However, chronicles of the Spanish expeditions through the interior in the 1500s recorded the indigenous Muskogean peoples' political titles derived from the Maya and Muskogean languages.

The high king of Apalache would have been called the *Hene-mako*, an Itaza Maya word meaning Great Sun. Lesser officials would have been called *Hene Ahau* (Sun Lord,) *mako* or *mikko* (town leader,) *orata* (one who makes things happen,) and *emale* (representative of a leader). Several of these Muskogean words do appear when de Laudonnière discussed interior tribes.

A large lake appears south of the Appalachian Mountains on all 17th century maps. The lake does not appear on 18th century maps after around 1715. There is no large, natural lake in central Georgia today. The former larger lake probably was Little Ocmulgee River Swamp. Both this swamp and the Okefenokee Swamp were shallow lakes, similar in appearance to Lake Okeechobee, until Native Americans were driven from their environs. Apparently, either the natural dam that created the lake washed out, or Native Americans had been keeping out vegetation by burning it off.

While the *Cofachites* were busie about the plundering and pillaging the houses they had found neer the great Lake, the *Apalachites* had the opportunity to prepare themselves for the reception of them: But the former, instead of taking the ordinary Roads and ways which led to the flat Country, which, as we said, lie between the Mountains, having left their wives and children neer the great Lake, under guard of some Forces they had drawn off from the main Body, and being guided by some of the *Apalachites*, whom they had surprised fishing in the great Lake, cros'd through the woods, and made their way over mountains and precipices, over and through which the Camels could hardly have pass'd, and by that means got into the heart and centre of the Country, and found themselves of a sudden in a province, called that of the *Amanites*: They without any resistance surpriz'd the chiefest places of it, wherein they found to guard them only Women, Children, and some old men, such as were not able to follow their King, who with his people lay expecting the Enemy at the ordinary descents which led into the Country.

The province of Amana was in the region once dominated by the large town now called Ocmulgee National Monument. The invasion could have occurred around 1150 AD, when the acropolis at Ocmulgee was abandoned. About 50 years later the first occupation of Etowah Mounds ended, when catastrophic floods sent the waters of the Etowah River over the town. The floods also covered the town of Ichese, which was two miles downstream from the Ocmulgee Acropolis. It is more probable, though, that Lake Tama was created at this time.

There was another period of apparent violence around 1375 AD. Etowah Mounds was sacked and burned. A new ethnic group appeared in the North Carolina Mountains. Much of the Savannah River Basin was abandoned at this time. The town of Ichese on the Ocmulgee River appeared to decline in importance.

When Hernando de Soto explored the Southeast in the spring of 1540, there was a no-man's land between the Itstate-Creek speaking province of Okute and a Muskogee-Creek speaking enemy province in South Carolina that was dominated by the town of Kofitachikee (Cofitachequi in Spanish.) The people of Okute greatly feared the raiders from across this no-man's land. These historical facts most closely match the description of the Cofachites by Rochefort.

❖

The *Cofachites* perceiving that their design had prov'd so successful, and that there was a great likelihood that in a short time they should become Masters of the whole Country, since they had met with so good fortune immediately upon their first appearance, prosecuted their conquests further, and having Cities for their retreat, where they had left good strong Garisons, they marched towards the King of *Apalacha*, with a resolution either to fight him, or at least oblige him to allow them the quiet possession of some part of the Country. The *Apalachite* was extremely surpriz'd, when he understood that the Enemy, whom he had all this while expected on the Frontiers, and at the known avenues of the Country, had already possess'd himself of a Province that lay in the center of his Dominions, and that he had left Garisons in the Cities and most considerable places thereof: However, being a magnanimous and gallant Prince, he would try whether the chance of Arms would prove as favorable to him, as he thought his cause good and just; he thereupon came down with his people out of the Mountains, where he had encamped himself; and having encourag'd those that were about him to do their utmost, he confidently set upon the vanguard of the *Cofachites*, which was come out to observe his motion: having on both sides spent all their arrows, they came to a close fight, and having taken their Clubs, there was a great slaughter in both Armies, till that night having separated them, the *Cofachites* observ'd that they had lost a great number of theirs in the engagement, and found that they had to do with a people that behav'd themselves more valiantly than they had imagined to themselves they would have done; and consequently that their best course would be to enter into a friendly treaty with them, rather than venture another hazard of their Forces in a strange Country.

Upon this they resolv'd, that the next morning they would send Embassadors to the King of the *Apalachites*, with certain Overtures of Peace, and in case of refusal (dissembling the loss they had receiv'd in the former Engagement) to declare open War, and to challenge him to be immediately ready to receive their Charge, which should be much more violent then what they had met withal the day before; and that then all their Forces were come together. The *Paracoussis* of the *Apalachites* having given audience to these Embassadours, desir'd that days time to consider of the Propositions which had been made to him; and thereupon having requir'd of them the Articles and Conditions under which they would Treat with him, in case he might be inclin'd to Peace, they told him, That they had left their own Country with a resolution to plant themselves either by friendship or by force in that good and fat Country whereof he was possess'd and that if he would condescend to the former of those means, they desired to become one People with the *Apalachites*, to dwell in their Country, and to cultivate it, and to supply the empty places of those who not long before had gone from among them to plant a new Colony in some remote parts of the World.

The *Apalachite* assembled his Council upon these considerations, and having acquainted them therewith, he represented, That the Army of the *Cofachites* hindred the coming in of the Assistances which they might receive from other Provinces that had not been ready to come in to them at the beginning of the War; That by the same means the passage of Provisions was absolutely obstructed; That the Enemy was Master of the Field, and that without any resistance he had got into one of the best Provinces of the whole Country, where he had also possess'd himself of places of Importance; and, That though in the precedant Engagement he had taken particular notice of the imcomparable fidelity and gallantry of his People, in setting upon and fighting against the Enemies, over whom they had very considerable Advantages, yet had that good Success been bought with the loss of his most valiant Captains, and the best of his Souldiers; and consequently it concern'd them to bethink themselves of some means to preserve the rest of the Kingdom, by sparing what was then left of the choicest Men: And since the

Enemies were the first Proposers of the Conditions of Peace, it would be the safest way to hearken thereto, if it might be done without any derogation from their Glory, and the great Reputation they had aquir'd before; inasmuch as there was waste grounds enough in several places, and that the Country, by reason of the transplantation of some part of their Inhabitants, was spacious and fertile enough to sustain them all.

All the chief Commanders of the *Apalachites* having heard what had been propos'd by their King, and concluding it was not fear that oblig'd him to hearken to an Accomodation with the *Cofachites*, since that the day before he had ventur'd his Person among the most forward; but that it proceeded purely from the desire he had that they might not be rashly expos'd to further danger, and his care of preserving his People, which was already at the mercy of the Enemy, who had possess'd himself of one of the richest Provinces; and having also understood by some Spies who were come into the King's Army by some secret ways, and made their escape out of the Cities where the *Cofachites* had their Garisons, that they treated with great mildness and respect the women and old men whom they had found there; having, I say, taken all these things into consideration, they unanimously subscribed to the sentiments of their Prince, and made answer, That there was a necessity of condescending to an Accomodation, and making some Agreement upon the most advantageous Conditions they could, according to the present posture of their Affairs: And after they had confirm'd this resolution by their *Ha Ha*, which is the sign of the applause and ratification wherewith they are wont to conclude their Deliberations, they signified the same to the Embassadors of the *Cofachites*, who expected it with impatience.

In the chronicles of the Juan Pardo Expedition (1567-1568) written by Juan de la Bandera, the Spaniards wrote down the word of approval as "ya." The word is actually "hiya" and is still sung in the Creek Stomp Dance and several ceremonies.

The news being carried over to the Camp of the *Cofachites*, was receiv'd with great joy, as being consonant to the end they had propos'd to themselves when they first undertook the War and left their Country: They thereupon immediately deputed some of the chiefest among them to agree with the *Apalachites* about the absolute conclusion of that Peace, and to sign the Articles of the Treaty. These deputies being come to the place where the Prince of the *Apalachites* expected them, attended by the most considerable Persons about his Court, sitting on a Seat somwhat higher than any of the rest, and covered with a rich Fur, were very kindly receiv'd; and having taken their Seats, the King drank to them of a certain Beverage call'd *Cassina*, out of a Bowl of which he first tasted himself: All that were present at the Council drank afterwards in order; which done, they fell upon the business of the Treaty, which was concluded upon these Conditions;

That the *Cofachites* should inhabit promiscously in the Cities and Towns of the *Apalachites*; That in all respects they should be esteem'd and accounted as the natural Inhabitants of the Country; That they should absolutely enjoy the same Priviledges; That they should be subject to the King, as the others were; That they should embrace the Religion, and observe the Customs of the Country: Or if they would rather, the *Apalachites* would resign them the rich and great Province of *Amana*, to be enjoy'd only by them, according to the limits which should be agreed upon: Provided nevertheless That they should acknowledge the King of the *Apalachites* for their Sovereign, and that from thence forward they should render him reasonable homage.

This agreement being thus reciprocally concluded, was

attended with mutual acclamations: Not long after, the Deputies of the *Cofachites* having given an account of their negotiation to their Commander in Chief and his Councel, and represented to them the choice which had been left them either of living promiscuously among the *Apalachites*, or being sole possessors of the Province into which they were entered; they unanimously accepted the latter, and so became absolute Masters of that Province of *Amana*, whereof the King of the *Apalachites* put them himself into quiet possession: The Women, Children and Old men who had been left behind, when all such as were able to bear arms had follow'd their Prince, were transported into some of the other Provinces, where the King appointed a setled habitation for them, and all the gallant men of that Province who had ventur'd their lives against the Enemy, and for the Preservation of their Country.

All things being thus setled, both parties laid down their arms, and the *Cofachites* went to fetch their Wives, Children, Cattel, and the Souldiers they had left neer the great Lake of *Theomi*; and being safely return'd, they dispos'd themselves into the Cities appointed them, congratulating their good fortune in the conquest of so noble a Country, answerably to their expectation at the first undertaking of the War.

Apparently, the name of the lake in central Georgia was Tama. The Tamatli were later a major division of the Creek Confederacy. Some dialects in the region pronounced the word, Thama.

The Province of Cofita was in present day east central Georgia when visited by Hernando de Soto in 1540. However, the description of the Cofafhites seizing the heart of Apalache, indicates that they originally conquered the Lower Ocmulgee River Basin. A people from Puerto Rico, the Toa, were living in that region in 1540, when visited by Hernando de Soto.

From that time the *Apalachites* gave the name of *Carib-bians,* or as the French would have it, *Caraibes,* to those new comers, who of a sudden, and contrary to their expectation, forc'd themselves upon them, to repair the breach which had been made by the transplantation of some of their people into another Country of *America*: So that this word *Caraibes* signifies, in their language, a sort of *people added,* or *suddenly and unexpectedly coming in, strangers,* or *stout and valiant men*; as if they would express, that a generous people, whom they expected not, were come upon them, and had been added to them: and this denomination continu'd to these new comers instead of that of *Cofachites,* which hath been kept up only in some weak and wretched Families which liv'd more towards the north of *Florida,* and after the departure of the true *Cofachites,* possess'd themselves of their habitations, and would also have pass'd under the name of those who had preceded them in the possession of that Country: Whereas on the other side, these true *Cofachites* were known by the name of *Caribbians* in the Province of *Amana*; and there-fore henceforward we shall speak of them, and the Colonies which they have since sent abroad, only under that name.

These two Nations being thus united by the determina-tion of their differences, and the period they put to a cruel war which might have ruin'd them both, liv'd afterwards in good correspondence for many years. But in the process of time, the *Caribbians* finding themselves mulitply'd in the Country which they had conquer'd by their arms, would not embrace the Religion of the *Apalachites,* who ador'd the Sun, as shall be shewn hereafter, nor be present at their Cer-emonies in the Temple they had in the Province of *Bemarin,* where the Court was; nor in fine render the King the homag-es that were due to him for the Province they were possess'd of, according to their promise, and the Articles of the Treaty.

This breach of promise on the part of the *Caribbians,* and that unjustifiable act, prov'd the occasion of many bloudy

Wars which happen'd afterwards between the two Nations: the *Caribbians* were surrounded of all sides by their adversaries, who kept them in so, that they could not any way enlarge their quarters; and on the other side the *Apalachites* had in the bowels of their Country a cruel and irreconcileable enemy, who kept them perpetually in alarms, and oblig'd them to be always in arms; during which, both the one and the other, sometimes victorious, sometimes beaten, as the uncertain chance of war was pleas'd to carry it, liv'd a very sad life; insomuch that, many times, either for want of cultivating the ground, or by reason of the waste committed in the fields of one another, a little before the Harvest, they were reduc'd to such an extreme Famine, as destroy'd more people than the Sword.

Above an age was spent in these contests, during which the *Caribbians*, who had for their Commander in Chief and King of their Nation, one of their most valiant Captains, whom they called *Ragazim*, added to their former acquests another Province, which lay next to them on the South Side, and is called *Matica*, which reaching through the Mountains by an interval that receives a torrent descending from the same Mountains, afterwards extends towards the West, as far as the River, which taking its source at the great Lake, after it hath made several Islands, and flown through divers Provinces, falls at last into the Ocean: This is the famous River which the French have called the River of *May*; but the *Apalachites* name it *Basainim*, which signifies in their language, *the delicious River*, or *abounding in fish*. The *Caribbians* having thus dilated their territories, and forc'd their Enemies to retreat, made for some years a truce with the *Apalachites*, who being wearied out with the Wars, and discourag'd by the loss of a considerable Province, willingly hearkened to that cessation of arms, and all acts of hostility.

The May and Basainim Rivers are one and the same

as the Ocmulgee-Altamaha River system. In south central Georgia, the Ocmulgee is joined by the Oconee River to form the Altamaha. The word Altamaha is the Anglicization of the Itza Maya words, Al Tama Ahau, which mean, "Place of the Merchant Lord."

The Cofitachite's apparently conquered the Upper Ocmulgee River Basin. The sources of the Ocmulgee are in the southeastern and eastern suburbs of Atlanta. Approximately, a century ago, an Arawak hilltop shrine was discovered near the confluence of Sweetwater Creek and the Chattahoochee River. At the shrine was found a stone stela with a Caribbean demon god on it.

But these *Apalachites* being exasperated to see their Country grown less by one of the best Provinces belonging to it, taking the advantage of the opportunity of that Truce, secretly consulted several times among themselves how they might carry on their designs more successfully against the *Caribbians* then they had done before; and having found by sad experience, that they had not advanced their affairs much by assaulting their Enemies openly, and by setled Engagements, they resolv'd to supplant them by subtlety, and to that end to think of all ways imaginable to make a division among them, and insensibly to engage them in a Civil War within their own Country. This advice being receiv'd and generally approv'd of all their Priests, who are in very great esteem among them, and have Voices in their most important Assemblies, immediately furnish'd them with expedients, and suggested to them the means which were to this effect. They had observ'd that those people who came in so slily and surpriz'd them in their own Country, were without Religion, and made no acknowledgment of any Divinity, whereto they conceiv'd themselves oblig'd to render any publick Service, and that they stood in fear only of a certain

Sweetwater Creek Stela

Four feet tall stone stela, found near Atlanta, GA that portrays the Caribbean demon god.

evil Spirit which they called *Mabouya*, because he sometimes tormented them; yet so as that in the mean time they did not do him any homage: Thence it came that for some years after their arrival, during which they had liv'd in good correspondence with them, they endeavour'd to induce them by their example to acknowledge the Sun to be the sovereign Governour of the World, and to adore him as God.

❖

This paragraph precisely describes the culture and religion of the Carib Indians, who feared (more than worshiped) the demon god, Mabouya. Today, the word Mabouya is better known as the name of a type of harmless lizard that lives in the Antilles.

❖

These Exhortations and Instructions had a great influence over the Spirits of the chiefest among the *Caribbians*, and had made strong impressions in them; so that having receiv'd the first Principles of that Religion while the time of their mutual correspondence continu'd, many left the Province of *Amana* wherein they had their habitations, and went into that of *Bemarin*, the principal Province of the *Apalachites*, whence they ascended into the Mountain of *Olaimi*, upon which the Apalachites made their solemn Offerings; and upon their invitation the *Caribbians* had participated of those Cermonies and that Service: These Priests, whom the Apalachites call *Jaouas,* which is as much as to say, *Men of God,* knew that the seeds of Religion are not so easily smother'd in the hearts of men; and that, though the long Wars they had had with the *Caribbians* had hinder'd the exercise thereof, yet would it be no hard matter for them to blow up, as we may say, those sparks in them which lay hid under the ashes.

The Truce and Cessation of all acts of Hostility, which had been concluded between the two Nations, presented the *Apalachites* with a favorable opportunity to prosecute their design; whereupon the Priests of the Sun advis'd, with the Kings Consent, that there should be a publication made among the *Caribbians*, that at the beginning of the month of March, which they call *Naarim* in their language, they would render a solemn Service in honour of the Sun, on the high Mountain; and that the said Service should be attended with Divertissements, Feasting, and Presents, which they should liberally give to such as were present thereat. This Ceremony was no new thing among the *Apalachites*, so that the *Caribbians* could not suspect any circumvention, nor fear any surprise; for it was a very ancient custom among them to make extraordinary Prayers to the Sun at the beginning of the Month of *Naarim*, which is precisely the time that they have done sowing their *Mais*. That which they desire in this Service is, That the Sun would be pleas'd to cause that which they had recommended to his care, to spring, grow, and come to maturity. They have also the same solemnity in the Month of *May*, at which time they have got in their first Harvest, to render him thanks for the fruits they conceive that they have receiv'd from his hands. Besides, the *Caribbians* knew well enough, that during these Festivals the *Apalachites* hung up their Bows and Arrows; that it was accounted a hainous crime among them to go arm'd into their Temple, and to raise the least dispute there; and that during those days of Selemnity, the greatest Enemies were commonly reconcil'd, and laid aside all enmity. In fine, they made not the least doubt but that the Publick Faith, and the Promise solemnly made, would be inviolably observ'd.

In this paragraph Rochefort seemed to describe the Green Corn Festival. However, that festival occurred at the end of the Muskogean year in a four or five day period prior to the Summer Solstice in June.

The length of the festival was determined by the astronomer priests, who calculated how many leap days were required to keep the solar calendar accurate.

❖

Upon the assurance they dispose themselves to pass over into the Province of *Bemarin* at the time appointed; and that they might be thought to contribute somwhat on their part to the publick Solemnity, they dress themselves will all the bravery and magnificence they could; and though that even then they were wont to go very lightly clad, and expose their bodies almost naked, yet the more to accomodate themselves to the humours of their Neighbours, whom they were going to visit, they caused all the Furs, Spotted Skins, and Stuffs that they had, to be made into Cloaths: They forgot not also to cause their faces, their hands, and all those places of their bodies which lay expos'd to be seen, to be painted with a bright red; and they crown themselves with their richest Garland, interwoven with the different plumage of several rare Birds of the Country. The Women for their parts, desirous to participate of this Solemnity, leave nothing undone that might contribute any thing to the adorning of themselves; the Chains of Shells of several colours, the Pendants, and the high Coifs enrich'd with the precious and glittering Stones which the Torrents bring down along with them out of the Mountains, made them appear with extraordinary lustre. In this equipage the *Caribbians*, partly out of curiousity, partly out of the vanity to shew themselves, and some certain motives of Religion, undertake that Pilgrimage: And that they might not raise any jealousie in those who had so kindly invited them, they leave their Bows, Arrows, and Clubs at the last Village within their Jurisdiction, and enter into the Province of *Bemarin* only with a walking stick, singing and dancing, as they are all of a merry and divertive disposition.

On the other side, the *Apalachites* expected them with

great devotion, and answerably to the Orders they had to that purpose receiv'd from their King, whose name was *Teltlabin*, and whose race commands at present among that people; they kindly entertain'd all those who came to the Sacrifice; nay, from the first entrance of the *Caribbians* into their Province, they treated them at all places as cordially as if they had been their Brethern, and that there had never been any difference between them: They seated them all along the way, and conducted them up to the Royal City, which to this day they call *Melilot*, that is, *City of Councel*, inasmuch as it is the habitation of the King and his Court: The chiefest of the *Caribbians* were magnificently entertain'd at the Palace-Royal, and those of the common sort were receiv'd and treated by the Inhabitants of the City, who spar'd no cost to heighten the satisfaction of their Guests.

The day dedicated to the sacrifice of the Sun being come, the King of the *Apalachites* with his Court, which was very much increas'd by the arrival of the *Caribbians*, and a great number of the Inhabitants of the other Provinces, who were come up to the Feast, went up very betimes in the morning to the top of the Mountain of *Olaimi*, which is not a full league distant from the City: This Prince, according to the Custome of the Country, was carried in a chair, on the shoulders of four tall men, attended by four others of the same height, who were to relieve the former when they were weary: There marched before him several persons playing on Flutes and other musical Instruments; with this pomp he came to the place appointed for the Assembly; and when the Ceremony was over, he made a great distribution of Cloaths and Furs, more than he had been accustomed to do upon such occassions before: But above all, his liberality was remarkable towards the most considerable persons among the *Caribbians*; and in imitation of the Prince, the wealthiest of his people made presents in like manner to those of that Nation who had vouchsafed their solemn Sacrifice with their presence; so that most of the

Caribbians return'd home well satisfy'd, and in better Liveries than they had brought thence with them: After they were come down from the Mountain, they were again treated and entertain'd with the greatest expressions of good will, in all the houses of the *Apalachites*, through whose habitations they were to return into their quarters: In fine, to encourage them to a second visit, there were solemn protestations made to them from the King and his Officers, that they should be at all other times receiv'd with the like demonstrations of affection, if they were desirous to accompany them four times in the year to the celebration of the same Ceremonies.

The *Caribbians* being returned into their Province could not make sufficient acknowledgments of the kind entertainment the had receiv'd: Those who had stay'd at home being ravish'd to see the rich presents which their Country-men had brought home, immediately resolv'd to undertake the same pilgrimage at the next ensuing Feast: And the day on which it was to be drawing neer, there was so great a contestation among them who should go, that if their *Cacick*, or chief Captain, had not taken some course therein, the Province would have been destitute of Inhabitants: The *Apalachites* on the other side continu'd their entertainments and liberalities; and there was a certain emulation among them who should be most kind to the *Caribbians*: Their Priests, who knew what would be the issue of all this imposture, recommended nothing so much to them, as the continuation of those good Offices, which they said were very acceptable to the Sun.

Three years slipp'd away in these visits; at the end whereof the *Apalachites,* who had exhausted themselves in liberalities towards their Neighbours, perceiving they had gain'd extreamly upon their affections, and that the greatest part of them were grown so zealous for the service of the Sun, that nothing would be able to force out of their apprehensions the deep sentiments they had conceiv'd of his Divinity; resolv'd, upon the instigation of their Priests, for whose advice the

King and all the people had great respects and submissions, to take occasion from the expiration of the Truce to renew the war against the *Caribbeans*, and to forbid them access to their Ceremonies, if they would not, as they did, make a publick profession of believing the Sun to be God, and perform the promise they had sometime made of acknowledging the King of the *Apalachites* for their Sovereign, and do homage to him for the Province of *Amana*, upon which account they had been admitted to be the Inhabitants thereof.

The *Caribbians* were divided about these proposals: For all those who were inclin'd to the adoration of the Sun, were of opinion, that satisfaction should be given to the *Apalachites*, affirming, that, though they were not oblig'd thereto by their promise, yet there would be an engagement to do it, though it were only to prevent their being depriv'd of the free exercise of their Religion, and debar'd their presence at the sacrifices made to the Sun, which they could not abandon without much regret: The *Cacick* or chief Commander, and a great number of the most considerable among the *Carribians* alledged on the contrary, that they would not blast their reputation, and the glory of all their precedent Victories, by so shameful a peace, which, under pretence of Religion, would make them subject to the A*palachites*; That they were freeborn, and that, as such, they had left the place of their birth and transplanted themselves into a better Country than their own, by force of Arms; That their greatest concernment was to endeavour the continuance of that precious liberty, and to cement it with their own blood, if occasion requir'd; That they were the same men who had sometime forc'd the *Apalachites* to resign up to them the most considerable of their Provinces, such a one as was the centre, and as it were the eye of their Country; That they had not remitted any thing of that generosity, and that that valor was so far from being extinguish'd, that on the contrary they had enlarged their jurisdiction by the acquest of a noble and spacious Country, which gave them passage beyond the Mountains, whereby they were surrounded before; That having thus remov'd out of the way whatever might obstruct their designs, it would be thought an insupportable cowardice in them, only under pretence of Religion, and out of pure curiousity at being present at Sacrifices, to quit the possession of what they had reduc'd under their power with so much trouble and bloodshed: In fine, that if any were desirous to adore the Sun, they needed not to go out of their own territiores to do it, since he shined as favorably in their Provinces as those of the *Apalachites*, and look'd on them every day as graciously as on any other part of the world; and if there were any necessity of consecrating a Mountain to him, or a Grot, they might find among those which separated their Country from the great Lake, some that were as high and as fit for those mysteries as that of *Olaimi*.

Those who maintained the service of the Sun, and were against engaging in a new war, which must be the sequel of refusing conditions which were as advantageous to them as to the *Apalachites*, made answer; that since they had for some years enjoy'd the sweetness of peace, and experienc'd upon so many occasions the kind entertainments and generosity of their Neighbours, it would be the greatest imprudence in the world to run themselves into new troubles, which they might avoid upon such easie terms, and that without any loss of the reputation they had acquir'd; That the acknowledgments which the *Apalachites* requir'd for the Province they were possessed of, might be such, and of so little importance, that it would not be any diminuition of the Honour, or prejudice to their Authority; That as to what concern'd the Service and Sacrifices of the Sun, they were not furnish'd with such Priests as were instructed in that Science, and acquainted with the Ceremonies thereof; That it was much to be fear'd that if they should undertake to imitate the *Jaoüas* of the *Apalachites*, they would, by the miscarriages likely to be committed therein, draw upon themselves the indignation of the

Divinity which they would serve, instead of gaining its favour; That they had found upon enquiry, that there was not any Mountain in the whole Country so kindly look'd upon by the Sun, and so pleasant as that of *Olaimi*: Nor was there any other that had a Temple naturally made in the Rock, after so miraculous a manner, which as such, that all the art and industry of man could never bring to that perfection, and that it could be no other than the work of the beams of that Divinity which was there ador'd; That though it were suppos'd they might find out a Mountain and a Cave that came somewhat neer the other, which yet they thought impossible, it was questionable whether those Birds who were the Sun's Messengers would make their habitation there; And that the Fountain consecrated in honour of him, which wrought admirable effects, and unheard of cures, would be found there; And consequently, that they would expose themselves to the derision of the *Apalachites*, who would still have occasion to make their brags of an infinite number of prerogatives peculiar to their ancient Temple and Service, which the new one they pretended to build would never have. From all which considerations the Religious party concluded, that their best course was to make a firm peace, that so they might have the convenience of participating of the same Ceremonies for the future, which they had frequented during the Truce.

But those who were resolv'd on the contrary side were so obstinate, that all those remonstrances prevail'd nothing upon them, nor could in the least divert them from the resolution they had taken never to acknowledge the *Apalachites* for their Sovereigns, nor lose their liberty under pretense of Religion and way of Worship, which their fore-fathers had been ignorant of: So that, in fine, this contrariety of sentiments made an absolute rupture among the *Caribbians*, so as to divide them into two factions, as the Priests of the *Apalachites* had foreseen; whereupon being divided also in their Councels, they could not return an unanimous answer to the propositions of peace or war which had been made to them by the *Apalachites*: But either party growing stronger and stronger daily, that which voted for an allyance with the *Apalachites*, and stood for the adoration of the Sun, became so powerful as to be in a condition to oblige the other either to embrace their opinion, or quit the Province.

It would be too tedious a Relation to set down here all the mischiefs and miseries which that Civil War brought among the *Caribbians*, who mutually destroy'd one the other, till at last, after many fights, the *Apalachites* joyning with that party which carried on their Interests, the other was forced to quit the Provinces of *Amana* and *Matica*, and to find out a more setled habitation elsewhere.

The victorious *Caribbians* having, by the assistance of the *Apalachites*, rid themselves of those who were the disturbers of their Peace, fortified their Frontiers, and placed up and down on the avenues the most valiant and most generous of their Forces, to deprive the Banish'd of all hope of ever returning: That done, they contracted a most strict Alliance with the *Apalachites*, submitting themselves to their Laws, embracing their Religion, and so making themselves one people with them; and that incorporation continues to this day; yet not so, but that those *Caribbians* do still retain their ancient name, as we have already observ'd in the beginning of this Chapter; as also many words which are common between them and the Inhabitants of the *Caribbies*: Of this kind are, among an infinite number of others, the terms of *Cakonnes*, to express the little curiosities which are preserv'd for their rarity; that of *Bouttou*, to signifie a Club of a weighty kind of wood; that of *Taumali*, to express a certain picquancy or delightfulness of taste; that of *Banaré*, to signify a familiar friend; that of *Etoutou*, to denote an Enemy: Thay also call a Bow, *Allouba*; Arrows, *Alouani*; a great Pond, *Taonaba*; the evil Spirit, *Mabouya*; and the Soul of a Man, *Akamboué*; which are the proper terms which the *Caribbian* Inhabitants of the

Islands make use of at the present to signifie the same things.

The words above were also used by the Caribs living in the Lesser Antilles and Dominica.

As concerning the *Caribbians* forc'd out of their Country by those of their own Nation, and driven out of the limits of their ancient Habitation, and all the places they had Conquer'd; having straggled up and down a while neer the River which derives its source from the great Lake, and endeavour'd to no purpose to enter into some Accomodation with the Inhabitants of either side of it, they at last resolv'd to make their way through their Country, either by fair means or foul, and so to get into some place where they might perpetuate themselves, and make a secure establishment of what was left of them: With this resolution they made a shift to get to the Sea-side, where having met with a people who took compassion on their misery, they winter'd among them, and passed over that disconsolate Season in much want: And while they spent their time in continual regrets, for their loss of a Country so pleasant and fertile as that which they had liv'd in, and considered that they should never enjoy themselves in that whereto their misfortune had cast them as Exiles, there arrived where they were, at the beginning of the Spring, two little Vessels, which came from the Islands called the *Lucayos,* and had been driven by the Winds into the Road neer which our *Caribbians* had pass'd over the Winter: There were in those two Vessels, which they call *Canows* or *Piragos*, about thirteen or fourteen persons, Inhabitants of *Cigateo*, one of the *Lucayan* Islands, who being got ashore, related to the natural Inhabitants of the Country how they had been forc'd thither by a Tempest; and among other things, they told wonders of the Islands where they liv'd, adding, that there were yet divers others beyond them, towards the Æquator, which lay desart, and were not inhabited, and those such as were accounted better then the others whereof they had given them an account: That for their parts, all they desired of the Inhabitants of the Country was only some Provisions, and a little fresh Water, to enable them to get home to their own Country, from which they conceiv'd themselves to be distant not above four or five days sailing.

The *Caribbians*, who were studying where to find out some new habitation, and extremely troubled that they had no setled place, where they might no longer be expos'd to the inconveniences of a wandering kind of life, having heard so much of these Islands, and that they were not far from the *Lucayas*, resolv'd to make their advantage of the opportunity of those Guides, whom they had met with by so extraordinary a good fortune, to follow them, when they should depart thence, and after their arrival at home, to plant themselves in some of those desart Islands whereof they had given advantagious an account.

This last section is interesting because it strongly contrasts with assumptions made by anthropologists over the past two centuries. It is an accepted fact among anthropologists that the Caribs were one of the bands of people who migrated northward from South America or Central America.

According to Rochefort, the people who gave their name to the Caribbean Sea actually were indigenous to Florida, but invaded Georgia. Wars between Carib provinces in Georgia forced the losers to invade the northern Antilles. The timing of the initial invasion may be around 1150 AD. That is when both the great town of Ocmulgee in central Georgia and a cluster of culturally related towns near Lake Okeechobee, FL were suddenly abandoned. Etowah

Mounds was temporarily abandoned about 50 years later. The archaeological records support Rochefort's story.

Chapter VIII

By way of Digression giving an account of the Apalachites, the Nature of their Country, their Manners, and their ancient and modern Religion

Since we have had occasion to speak so much concerning the *Apalachites*, and that above one half of the ancient *Caribbians*, after the expulsion of those among them who would not adore the Sun, have to this present made up one people and one Common-wealth with those *Apalachites,* it will be consonant to our design, especially since the subject thereof is rare and little known, if we give some account of the nature of their Country, and the most remarkable things that are in it; as also of the manners of the Inhabitants, the Religion they have had heretofore, and that which they profess at this day, as we have had the particulars thereof from the English, who have traded among them, and have not long since laid the foundation of a Colony in the midst of the noblest, and best known of their Province.

Although contemporary history references state that the earliest English settlement in southwestern Virginia and northeastern Tennessee occurred approximately in 1770, numerous 18th century documents, including John Mitchell's famous 1755 map of North America, state that colonization of the Holston and Cumberland River Valleys began before 1650. Rochefort's book presents the exact same information. His statement also tells us that the "Kingdom of Apalache" extended into southwestern Virginia.

The English settlers were preceded by at least 50 years by Sephardic Jewish colonists. Several ancient mines have been discovered in the vicinity of Murphy, NC,

Mitchell County, NC and the Toe River Valley, NC. A tree growing in a collapsed mine shaft in Tomatla, NC (near Murphy) was dated to 1600 AD. In 1673 AD, Virginia explorers James Needham and Gabriel Arthur visited a Spanish speaking town built out of brick, somewhere in southwestern Virginia or northeastern Tennessee. The town contained a church with a bell tower. They also observed wooden villages occupied by "Africans."

The territories of the *Apalachites* consist of six Provinces, whereof three are comprehended within that noble and spacious Vale which is encompass'd by the Mountains of the *Apalates*, at the foot whereof these people inhabit: The most considerable of those Provinces, and which lies towards the East, wherein the King keeps his Court, is called *Bemarin*: That which is in the midst, and as it were in the centre of the three, is called *Amani* or *Amana*: And the third of those which are within that Vale, is known by the name of *Matica*. True it is, that this last, which begins in the Vale, reaches a great way into the Mountains, nay goes yet much beyond, even to the South-side of the great Lake, which they call *Theomi*: The other Provinces are *Schama* and *Meraco*, which are in the *Apalatean* Mountains; and *Achalaques*, which is partly in the Mountains, and partly in the Plain, and comprehends all the Marshes and Fenny places, confining on the great Lake *Theomi*, on the North-side.

According to Rochefort, the Kingdom of Apalache covered a vast area of the Southeastern Highlands, Piedmont and Coastal Plain that corresponded to all of the original territory of the Creek Indians. This region would have included most of Georgia, western North Carolina, southeastern Tennessee, the Apalachicola River Basin in Florida, plus the upper Coosa River Basin of Alabama and the Lower Chattahoochee River Basin in Alabama. In archaeological terms, it encompassed the Lamar, Dallas and Pisgah Cultural Areas. The description specifically refers to hunter-gatherer groups in the more rugged North Carolina Mountains, who were probably Shawnee.

The great vale that Rochefort discussed is apparently the Chattahoochee River Valley, but the description of the landscape seems confused with the Great Appalachian Valley in northwest Georgia. A French league varied between provinces, but was in the range of 2 ½ miles. The Great Appalachian Valley is defined on both sides by mountains. The Chattahoochee Valley is not defined by mountains once it leaves the Nacoochee Valley.

The Chattahoochee was called the Apalache River by 16th century French explorers. This valley was traditionally considered the heart of the Creek Nation. The Chattahoochee begins on the slopes of Georgia's highest mountain, Brasstown Bald. Little more than a rushing mountain creek, it then tumbles down the Unicoi Gap through Helen, GA then turns eastward through the Nacoochee Valley. The dramatic Nacoochee Valley was created by a line of ancient volcanic cones that ran east to west across the Blue Ridge Mountains. Just past the Nacoochee Valley, the Chattahoochee turns southwestward and drops through a series of Class 6 and Class 5 rapids into the Chattahoochee Fault. The river stays in this fault as it crosses the State of Georgia diagonally to Columbus, GA.

In an earlier chapter, Rochefort stated that the Altamaha River, called the May River by 16th century French explorers, created a great lake near the Coastal Plain. He calls it Lake Thama. In fact, the Creek province of Tama was at the southern end of the Little Ocmulgee River Swamp in south-central Georgia. Both it and the Okefenokee Swamp were shallow lakes like Lake Okeechobee until the 1700s. Several branches of the Creek Indians pronounced Tama as "Thama."

The coasts of Georgia and South Carolina were not in Apalache. A subsequent chapter specifically states that most of the population of Apalache was too far from the sea to know the fishes of the sea.

The Country under the King of the *Apalachites* being thus divided into six Provinces, there are in it some Mountains of a vast extent and prodigious height, which are for the most part inhabited by a people living only upon what they get from hunting, there being great store of wild beasts in those Wildernesses: Besides which, there are also certain Vales, which are peopled by a Nation that is less barbarous, such as addicts it self to the cultivation of the earth, and is sustain'd by the fruits it produces: And lastly, there are abundance of Marshes and Fenny places, and a great Lake, whereof the Inhabitants are very numerous, maintaining themselves by fishing, and what little good ground they have furnishes them withall.

The three Provinces which are in the Vale, which, as we said in the precedent Chapter, is sixty leagues in length and about ten more in bredth, lie as it were in a Champion Country, save only, that in some places there are certain risings and eminences, on which the Towns and Villages are commonly built; many little Rivers, which descend from the mountains, and abound in Fish, cross it up and down in several places: That part of it which is not reduced to culture is well furnish'd with fair trees of an excessive height: For instance, there are *Cedars, Cypress, Pines, Oaks, Panamas*, which the French call *Saxafras*, and an infinite variety of others which have no proper names among us.

As concerning the Fruit-trees of this Country, besides Chestnut and Walnut-Trees, which grow naturally there, the

English who have planted themselves in those parts, as we shall relate more at large towards the end of this Chapter, have planted Orange-trees, sweet and sharp Citrons, Lemons, several sorts of Apples and Pears, and divers Stones, as of Plumbs, Cherries, and Apricocks, which have thriv'd and multiplied so, that in some places of this Country there are more *European* fruits then in any other part in *America*.

There is also good store of those lesser sorts of Trees which bear leaves or flowers of sweet scent, such as Laurel, Jessemine, Roses, Rosemary, and all those others that are so ornamental in the Garden: Nor is there any want of Pinks, Carnations, Tulips, Violets, Lillies, and all other Flowers which adorn Knots and Borders. Pot-herbs also, and all sorts of Pulse and Roots, thrive very well there: Citruls, Cucumbers, and Melons are common all Summer long, and as well tasted as those which grow in any part of the *Caribbies.*

Strawberries and Raspberries grow in the Woods without any culture: They have also Small-nuts, Gooseberries, and an infinite variety of other small Fruits, which in their degree contribute to the delight and refreshment of the Inhabitants.

The Wheat, Barly, Rie, and Oats which some sow'd there at several Seasons, and in different Soils, hath grown only to the blade; but in requital, there grows every where such abundance of small Millet, Lentils, Chick-pease, Fetches, and Mais, or Turkish Wheat, which are sown and harvested twice a year, that the Inhabitants of the Plain Country have enough to supply those who live towards the Mountains, who bring them in exchange several sorts of Furs. The lands that are sown with Turkish Wheat are enclos'd with Quick-set Hedges, planted on both sides with Fruit-trees, most whereof are cover'd with wild Vines, which grow at the foot of the Trees.

As to the Volatiles of this Country, there are Turkeys, Pintadoes, Parrots, Woodquists, Turtles, Birds of prey, Eagles, Geese, Ducks, Herons, white Sparrows, *Tonatzuli,* a kind of bird that sings as sweetly as the Nightingal, and is of excellent plumage; and abundance of other Birds commonly seen neer Rivers and in the Forests, quite different from those that are seen in other parts of the World.

The *Apalachites* have no knowledge at all of Sea-fish, as being at too great a distance from the Coasts; but they take abundance in the Rivers and Lakes, which are extreamly nourishing, of an excellent taste, and much about the bigness and in figure somwhat like our Pikes, Carps, Perches, and Barbels: They also take Castors and Bevers neer the great Rivers, Lakes, and Pools; they eat the flesh of them, and make Furs of the Skins, for Winter-caps and other uses.

There is no venemous creature nor any wild beast in the lower part of the Country; for the Inhabitants of the Mountains, who are expert Huntsmen, drive them into the Forests where they find them continual work and sport: So that the flocks of sheep, and herds of cattel and swine graze up and down the skirts of the Mountains without any body to look after them. But within the woods, and in the desarts, which are not much frequented by men, there are divers Monstrous and dangerous Reptiles, as also Bears, Tygers, Lions, Wolves, and some other kinds of cruel Beasts, which live by prey, and are particular to those Countries.

The men in these Countries are for the most part of high stature, of an Olive-colour, and well-proportion'd, their hair black and long: Both men and women are very neat and curious in keeping their hair clean and handsomely order'd: the women tie up theirs about the crown of the head after the form of a garland; and the men dispose theirs behind the ears: But on days of publick rejoicing, all have their hair loose, dishevel'd , and dangling over their shoulders; a fashion becomes them well. The inhabitants of those Provinces that lie towards and among the Mountains, cut off all their hair on the left side of the head, that so they may the more easily draw their Bows, and they order that which grows on the other side, so as to make a crest standing over the right ear: Most of them wear neither Caps nor any thing instead of shoes, but they cover the body with the skins of Bears or Tygers, neatly sown together, and cut after the fashion of close coats, which reach down to their knees, and the sleeves are so short that they come not over the elbow.

The Inhabitants of the other Provinces which are seated in the Vales and Plains, went heretofore naked from the Navel upwards, in the Summer-time, and in Winter, they wore garments of Furrs; but now both men and women are clad all the year long: In the hottest seasons, they have light cloaths, made of cotton, wooll, or a certain herb, of which they make a thred as strong as that of Flax: The women have the art of spinning all these materials, and weaving them into several kinds of stuffs, which are lasting, and delightful to the eie. But in the winter, which many times is hard enough, they are all clad in several kinds of skins, which they have the skill to dress well enough: They leave the hair on some, and so make use of them as Furs: They have also the art of tanning Ox-hides, and other skins, and making Shoes and Boots of them.

The previous chapter confirmed what was said by the chroniclers of the de Soto Expedition. The indigenous peoples, who were ancestral to the Creek Indians, knew how to weave cloth. The flax-like cloth described by Rochefort was woven from Mulberry tree bark fibers. Other fabrics were woven from thistle, cottonwood and hemp fibers. By the time that English settlers arrived in the interior, most people had apparently forgotten how to weave cloth.

The men wear Caps made of Otter-skins, which are perfectly black and glittering, pointed before, and set out behind with some rich feathers, which hanging down over their Shoulders make them look very gracefully: But the women have no other ornament about the head, but what is deriv'd from the several dresses of their hair: They make holes in their ears, and wear pendants of Chrystal, or made of a certain smooth stone they have, which is of as bright a green as that of an Emrald: Of the same materials, they also make great Necklaces, which they wear when they would appear in state: They make great account of Corral, Chrystal, and yellow Amber, which are brought to them by Strangers; and they are only the Wives of the principal Officers that have Bracelets and Necklaces made of them: Though there be some *Spanish* and *English* Families among them, yet have they not alter'd any thing either as to their Cloaths or Course of Life.

This statement confirms that there were both Spanish-speaking and English-speaking colonists in the southern Appalachians by 1653. Most were probably in northeastern Tennessee, but there was a large European village in the Nacoochee Valley of Georgia throughout the 1600s.

The ordinary sort of people wear only a close coat without sleeves, over a thin garment of Goat-skins, which serves them for shirts: The Coat which comes down to the calf of the leg, is ty'd about the wast with a leathern girdle, which is set out with some little embroidery: But the Officers and heads of Families wear over that a kind of short Cloak, which covers only the back and the arms, though behind it falls down to the ground: This Cloak is fasten'd with strong leathern points, which make it fast under the neck, and lye close to the shoulders: The womens garments are of the same fashion with those of the men, save that those of the former come down to the ankles, and the Cloak hath two open places on the sides, though which they put forth their arms.

The previous paragraph is interesting because it clearly shows that the famous Creek Longshirt pre-dates the introduction of European fabrics. It also confirms what archaeologists had suspected from the discovery of ornate cloth in royal burials. The elite wore patterned cloth garments, while the commoners usually wore clothing made of softened leather.

To keep themselves clear of Vermine, they often wash their bodies with the juice of a certain root, which is of as sweet a scent as the *Flower-de-luce* of Florence, and hath this further vertue, that it makes the nerves more supple, and fortifies and causes a smoothness all over the body, and communicates an extraordinary delightful scent thereto.

The Cities of the three Provinces that are in the spacious Plain, which is at the foot of the Mountains, are encompassed on the outside by a large and deep Moat, which on the inside, instead of wals, is all planted with great posts pointed at the top, thrust a good depth into the ground; or sometimes with quick-set hedges intermixt with very sharp thorns; they are commonly about five or six foot in bredth: The Gates are small and narrow, and are made fast with little pieces of wood, which lie cross between small ramperts of earth that are on both sides, and which command the avenues: there are commonly but two Gates to every City; to enter in at them, a man must pass over a bridge so narrow, that two men cannot well march on a front upon it: The Bridge is built upon piles, which sustain certain planks, which they draw up in the night when they fear the least trouble.

The description of the Apalache towns is exactly what archaeologists unearthed at Etowah Mounds National

Landmark in northwest Georgia. These detailed descriptions give great credence to Rochefort's book.

It is seldom seen that there is above one City in every Province; nay there are some that have not above eight hundred houses in them: The Metropolis of the Country, which is called *Melilot*, hath above two thousand; they are all built of pieces of wood planted into the ground and joined one to another: The covering is for the most part of the leaves of reeds, grass, or rushes: Those of the Captains are done over with a certain Mastick, which keeps off the rain, and preserves the thatch from decaying in many years: The floors of all the houses is of the same material, whereto they add a certain golden sand which they get out of the neighbouring Mountains, and which gives such a lustre as if they were sown with little spangles of Gold.

The construction of the commoners' houses as described by Rochefort exactly matches the post-ditch type houses unearthed by archaeologists in the Lower Southeast. The mastic that he described was apparently pine rosin, but this is not certain. The golden sand that he described was mica and iron pyrate, which strengthened the clay stucco and made it appear to sparkle like gold. Near the coast, crushed shells were added to a stucco that included crude lime. The people of northern Florida told Hernando de Soto that the buildings in Apalache were coated with gold. They were obviously referring to the golden mica and fool's gold finish of the clay stucco.

The Rooms of the ordinary sort of people are hung only with a kind of Mat, made of Plantane-leaves and rushes, which they have the art of dying into several colours; those of persons considerable among them, are hung with precious Furs, or Deer-skins painted with divers figures, or with a kind of Tapistry made of Bird-feathers, which they so industriously intermingle, that it seems to be embroidered: Their Beds are about a foot and a half from the ground, and are cover'd with skins that are dress'd, and as soft as can be wish'd: These skins are commonly painted with Flowers, Fruits, and a hundred such inventions, and their colours are so well set on and so lively, that at a distance one would take them for rich Tapistry: The wealthier sort in the winter time have their beds covered with the skins of Martins, Beavers, or white Foxes, which are so well dress'd, and perfumed with such artifice, that they never admit anything of ordure: The Officers and all the most considerable Inhabitants lie on Mattresses fill'd with a certain down that grows on a little plant, and is as soft as silk; but the common people take their rest on dry'd fern, which hath the property of taking away the weariness of the body, and retriving the forces exhausted by hunting, gardening, and all other painful exercises consequent to their course of life.

The ancestors of the Creek Indians wove baby clothes, elite women's blouses and women's undergarments from the fibers of the milk thistle. These fibers were evidently also used to fill mattresses slept on by the elite. Dried ferns were used by the commoners.

The Vessels they use in their houses are either of wood or earth, enamel'd with divers colours, and very delightfully painted: They sharpen upon stones the teeth of several wild beasts, and therewith arm their Arrows and Lances: Before strangers came among them and traded in their Country, they knew not there was such a thing as Iron; but they made use of extraordinary hard and sharp stones, instead of wedges, and certain smooth and cutting bones, instead of knives.

They all live amicably together under the conduct of a King, who keeps his Court at *Melilot*, the Metropolis of the Kingdome: In every City there is a Governour, and other subordinate Officers, who are appointed by him, and chang'd at his pleasure, as he thinks most convenient: the Villages also have Captains and heads of Families, by whom they are governed. All immoveable goods are common among these people, and excepting only their houses, and the little gardens belonging to them, they have no propriety in any thing: they carry on the business of Agriculture in common, and they share the fruits of the earth among themselves: At sowing-time the Governours and their Officers oversee the work; and at that time all those who are of age to do anything abroad, go out betimes in the morning to their work, and continue there till the evening, at which time they return to their Towns and Villages to take their rest: While they are at work, it is the business of their Chiefs to provide them somewhat extraordinary in meat and drink: They dispose their Harvest into the Publick Granaries, which are in the midst of their Towns and Villages; and at every full Moon, and at every new Moon, those who are entrusted with the distribution thereof, supply every Family, according to the number of persons whereof it consists, with as much as will suffice.

The description of public granaries matches those of the de Soto Expedition. The people grew their own vegetables and potatoes, however. Only corn was stored in bulk and rationed communally.

They are a temperate people, and hate all kinds of voluptuousness, and whatever tends to effiminency: And though Vines grow naturally in their Country, yet do they not make any wine but what is requisite for the divine service: Fair wa-

DETAIL OF ENGRAVING OF MELILOT

ter is their ordinary drink, but at great entertainments, they make use of a pleasant kind of Beer, which is made of *Turkey*-wheat: They also have the art of making an excellent kind of Hydromel, or Mead, which they keep in great earthen vessels: The great abundance of honey which they find among the Rocks, and in the clefts of hollow trees, supplies them with that whereof they make that delicious drink, which is such as may well pass for Sack, especially after it hath been kept a long time.

In an earlier paragraph, Rochefort referred to both maize and Turkey wheat. However, during the time of the earliest European contacts with the Americas the term Turkey wheat was applied to maize, i.e. Indian corn. He may be referring to indigenous cereals such as amaranth, Little Barley, sumpweed or goosefoot.

Virtually all biology books state that the honey bee is indigenous to the Old World and therefore Native Americans did not have honey. Anthropology books will state that the Mayas domesticated an indigenous, stingless honey bee and ate the honey it produced. The De Soto Chronicles stated that the only region where they observed domesticated honey bees and honey being consumed was in the province of Chiaha. Chiaha is an Itza Maya word meaning, "Salvia River" or "Lord of the Salvia" or "Beside the River." Locations of accent marks would change the meaning.

In contrast, the memoir of the commander of Fort Caroline (1564-1565), René de Laudonnière, stated that the elite of the coastal tribes of the Port Royal Sound, SC area consumed honey, presumably imported from the interior of the Southeast. Chiaha was in the kingdom of Apalache. Obviously, the ancestors of the Creek Indians consumed honey. It is not known if they raised the Maya honey bees or if somehow, Eurasian honey bees found their way to the Southeast.

Those of the same Family live so lovingly together, that there are among them some houses where an old man hath his children, and his children's children, to the third, nay sometimes to the fourth generation, all living under the same roof, to the number of a hundred persons, and sometimes more. Most of the other Nations of the Septentrional part of *America* who inhabit along the Sea-coast, are so slothful, that in the winter time they are in great want, because they had not sown anything when the time served, or had consumed the fruits of the precedent harvest in extraordinary entertainments and debauches: But the *Apalachites* hate nothing so much as idleness, and they are so addicted to pains-taking, that the fruits of the earth, being answerable to their labour, and being distributed with prudence and moderation, maintain them plentifully, nay so that they can, in case of necessity, assist their Neighbours the Inhabitants of the Mountains: Both men and women are perpetually employ'd, after feed-time and harvest, in spinning of Cotton, Wooll, and a certain Herb, which is soft and strong, for the making of cloth, and several ordinary sorts of stuffs wherewith they cover themselves: Some among them employ themselves in making of earthen ware; others in making Tapistry of the plummages of Birds; others, in making of Baskets, Panniers, and other little pieces of houshold-stuff, which they do with a strange industry.

They are a very loving and obliging disposition: And whereas their distance form the Sea exempts them from being subject to receive any displeasure from Strangers, they are in like manner ignorant what entertainments to make them, when they chance to visit them, and are never weary of expressing all manner of friendship towards them: They are docible and susceptible of all sorts of good disciplines; but they have this discommendable in them, that

101

they are very obstinate in their opinions, easily angered, and much addicted to revenge, when they are convinc'd that they have been injur'd: They are extreamly apt to give credit to their dreams, and they have some old dotards among them, who openly make it their business to interpret them, and foretell what things shall happen after them.

They have had a long continuance of peace; however they think it prudence to stand always upon their guard, and they have always Sentinels at the avenues of their Cities, to prevent the incursions of a certain savage and extreamly cruel people, which hath no setled habitation, but wander up and down the Provinces with an incredible swiftness, making havock whereever they come, especially where they find no resistance.

The Arms of the *Apalachites* are, the Bow, the Club, the Sling, and a kind of great Javelin, which they dart out of their hands, when they have spent all their Arrows: And whereas those that inhabit towards the woods and in the Mountains, live only by hunting, continual exercise makes them so expert in shooting with a Bow, that the King, who alwaies hath a Company of them about his person, hath no greater diversion than to see them shoot at a mark for some prize, which he gives him who in fewest shots came to the place assign'd, or hath shot down a Crown set up upon the top of a Tree.

They are passionate lovers of Musick, and all instruments that make any kind of harmony, insomuch that there's very few among them but can play on the Flute, and a kind of Hawboy, which being of several bigness, make a passably good harmony, and render a sound that is very melodious: They are mightily given to dancing, capering, and making a thousand postures, whereby they are of opinion they disburthen themselves of all their bad humours, and that they acquire a great activity and suppleness of body, and a wonderful swiftness in running. They heretofore celebrated solemn dances at the end of every harvest, and after they had made their Offerings to the Sun upon the Mountain of *Olaimi*; but now they have no set and appointed time for these divertisements.

Mount Olaimi was probably Brasstown Bald, GA, but may have been nearby Coosa Bald, Blood Mountain or even Yonah Mountain.

Their voice is naturally good, mild, flexible, and pleasant; whence it comes that many among them make it their endeavour to imitate the singing and chirping of Birds; wherein they are for the most part so fortunate, that like so many *Orpheus's* they entice out of the woods to follow them, those Birds which think they hear only those of their own species: They do also by singing alleviate the hard labour they are addicted unto, and yet what they do, seems to be done rather out of divertisement, and to avoid idleness, than out of any consideration of advantage that they make thereof.

Their Language is very smooth, and very plentiful in comparisons: That spoken by the Captains and all persons of quality, is more elegant and fuller of flourishes than that of the common sort of people: Their expressions are very precise, and their periods short enough: While they are yet children, they learn several songs, made by the *Jaouas* in honour and commendation of the Sun; they are also acquainted with several other little pieces of Poetry, wherein they have comprehended the most memorable exploits of their Kings, out of a design to perpetuate the memory thereof among them, and the more easily transmit it to their posterity.

The name of the priesthood is curious because it does not coincide with the known names for priests in the Muskogean or Maya languages. It is remarkably similar to the Elizabethan word for a Jew.

All the Provinces which acknowledge the King of *Apalacha* for their Sovereign, understand the language commonly spoken in his Court; yet does not this hinder but that each of them hath a particular dialect of its own, whence it comes that the language of some, is in some things different from that of others of the Inhabitants: The Provinces of *Amana* and *Matica*, in which there are to this day many *Caribbian* Families, have retained to this present many words of the ancient idiome of these people, which confirms what we have laid down for a certain assertion, to wit, that being known by the same name, and having many expressions common to them with the Inhabitants of the *Caribby*-Islands, those Families have also the same origine with them, as we have represented in the precedent chapter.

They heretofore adored the Sun, and had their Priests, whom they called *Jaouas*, who were very superstitious in rendring to him the service which they had invented in honour of him: their perswasion was, that the raies of the Sun gave life to all things; that they dried up the earth; and that once the Sun having continued four and twenty hours under an eclipse, the earth had been overflown; and that the great Lake which they call *Theomi*, was rais'd as high as the tops of the highest Mountains that encompass it; but that the Sun having recovered the eclipse, had, by his prefence, forc'd the waters to return into their abysses; that only the Mountain dedicated to his honour, and wherein his Temple was, was preserv'd from that deluge; and that their Predecessors, and all the beasts which are at present in the woods and upon the earth, having retir'd to the said Mountain, were preserv'd for the repopulation and recruit of the whole earth: So that they conceive themselves to be the most ancient people of the world; And they affirm, that from that time they had acknowledg'd the Sun for their God.

TONATZULI
(PAINTED BUNTINGS)
AT GREAT COPAL

THE TONATZULI
WERE CONSIDERED
BY THE APALACHE
TO BE
MESSENGERS OF GOD

Illustration by Richard L. Thornton

This story is remarkably similar to the story of the Great Flood and Noah's Ark.

They were of opinion, that the Sun had built himself the Temple which is in the Mountain of *Olaimi*, the ascent whereof is distant from the City of *Melilot* somewhat less that a league; and that the *Tonatzuli* (which are certain little birds about the bigness of a Quail, and whose bellies and wings are of a bright yellow, the back of sky-colour, and the head of a plumage partly red, and partly white) are the messengers and children of the Sun, which alwaies celebrate his praises.

Rochefort appears to be describing a Painted Bunting.

The service they rendered the Sun consisted in saluting him at his rising, and singing hymns in honour of him: They observed the same Ceremonies also in the evening, entreating him to return, and to bring the day along with him: And besides this daily service which everyone performed at the door of his house, they had also another publick and solemn service, which consisted in sacrifices and offerings, and was performed by the *Jaouas*, four times in the year, to wit, at the two feed-times, and after the two harvests, upon the Mountain of *Olaimi*, with great pomp, and a general concourse of all the Inhabitants of the six Provinces.

This Mountain of *Olaimi* is seated, as we have said before, in the Province of *Bemarin*, about a league distant from the Royal City of *Melilot;* but there is about another league of ascent and winding from the foot of it: It is certainly one of the most pleasant and most miraculous Mountains in the world: Its figure is perfectly round, and the natural descent extream steepy; but to facilitate the access thereof to such as are to go up, they have cut a good broad way all about it, and there are here and there several resting places gain'd out of the Rock, like so many neeches: All the circumference of it, from the foot to within two hundred paces of the top, is naturally planted with goodly trees of *Saxafras, Cedar*, and *Cypress*, and several others from which there issue *Rosins,* and *Aromatick gums,* of a very delightful scent: On the top of it there is a spacious plain, smooth and eaven all over, and somewhat better that a league in compass; it is covered with a delightful green livery of a short and small grass, which is intermixt with Thyme, Marjoram, and other sweet smelling herbs: And it was upon the top of the Mountain, and upon this pleasant verdure that the people stood, while the Priests of the Sun performed the divine service.

There is no major mountain in the Southern Highlands that is perfectly round. However, there are some smaller extinct volcanic cones in Union and White Counties, GA that approximate this description.

The place which serv'd them for a Temple, is a large and spacious Grott, or Cave, which is naturally cut in Rock, on the East-side of the Mountain: It hath a vast and large mouth, as the entrance of a magnificent Temple; As soon as the Sun is risen, he darts his rays on that entrance, which hath before it a fair and spacious square place, which a many would say were made by art in the Rock: And there it is that the *Jaouas*, the Priests of the Sun, stay expecting his rising to begin their ordinary Ceremonies of Festival Days. This Cave within is oval, two hundred foot in length, and proportionably broad; The Vault, which is naturally cut in the

Rock, rises up circularly from the ground to about a hundred foot high: There is just in the midst of it a great hole, or Lanthorn, which enlightens it from the top of the Mountain: This Lanthorn is emcompass'd with great stones, laid close together to prevent peoples falling in: The Vault on the inside is perfectly white, and the surface is covered with a certain *salt-peter*, which a man might take for white Coral diversy'd into several different figures; the whole compass of it is of the same lustre: the floor of it is also extremely eaven and smooth, as if it were all of one piece of marble. In fine, the greatest ornament of this Temple consists in its perfect whiteness; At the bottom of it there is a great Basin or Cistern, just over against the entrance, which is full of a very clear water, which perpetually distilling out of the Rock, is receiv'd into that place. Just in the middle of this Temple, directly under the Lanthorn which enlightens it, there is a great Altar all of one stone, of a round figure, three foot in height from the floor, and sustain'd by a short pillar, which Altar and the Pedestal seem to have been cut out of the place where it stands, that being in all probablity a piece of Rock which jutted out upon the floor of that miraculous Cave.

This temple was clearly not located in the Track Rock Terrace Complex in Union County, GA. The ruins of its temple face the Winter Solstice Sunset, not the Summer Solstice Sunrise. However, there is another large, mountainside archaeological zone with stone ruins in Union County that does face the sunrise. It is visible from the top of the Track Rock ruins.

Creek temples were traditionally stuccoed with a mixture of white kaolin clay and crushed shells. This is probably the white substance that Rochefort described.

GREAT COPAL

The Sacrifices which the *Jaouas* offered to the Sun, consisted not in the effusion of mans blood, or that of some certain beasts; for they were of a perswasion, that the Sun, giving life to all things, would not be pleas'd with a service that should deprive those creatures of a life which he had bestow'd on them; but the Sacrifice consisted only in Songs, which they had compos'd in honour of him, as also in the perfumes of certain aromatical drugs, which they appointed to be burnt on his Altar, and in the offering of garments, which the rich presented by the hands of the Priests, to be afterwards distributed among the poorer sort of people.

Creek Indian tradition is that their founders were refugees from an evil land where human sacrifice was practiced. Therefore, it was forbidden in Creek religions. The Spanish traders, who visited the Province of Apalache in the late 1500s called its mountainside capital, Great Copal. This apparently was in reference to the incense burned in the temples. A species of the copal plant has become feral in the region around the old capital of Apalache. It was used a pain killer by early frontier families, but now only grows at the edge of pastures near small streams.

All this Ceremony, which was performed four times a year, lasted from Sun-rising till noon, at which time the Assembly was dismiss'd: The Priests went up to the Mountain on the Eve of every Festival, to prepare themselves for that solemn Action; and the people, which came thither from all the Provinces, were there present some time before Sun-rising. The way which led up to the Mountain was enlightened by great Fires, which were kept in all that Night, for the convenience of those who went thither to adore. All the people remain'd without upon the Mountain, and none but the Priests durst come neer the Grot, which serv'd them for a Temple. Those who brought any Garments to be distributed to the poor, presented them to the Priests who stood at the entrance, and they hung them on the Poles which were on both sides of the Portal, where they remained till after the Service, and then they were distributed among the poor, as were also the other presents which the rich offered, and which were in like manner kept till the same time: Those also who brought Perfumes to burn on the Altar, deliver'd their presents to the Priests.

As soon as the Sun began to appear, the Priests who stood before the Temple began their Songs and Hymns, adoring him several times on their knees; then they went one after another to cast the Incense and Perfume which they had in their hands upon the Fire, which they had before kindled on the Altar, as also upon a great Stone which stood before the entrance of the Grot: This Ceremony being ended, the chiefest of the Priests powr'd some Honey into a hollow Stone, made somwhat like those Stones wherein the Holy-water stands in some places, which Stone stood also before this Temple; and into another, which was of the same figure and the same matter, he put some corns of *Turkey*-wheat a little bruis'd, and destitute of their outward Shell, as also some other small grains, which the Birds consecrated to the Sun, called *Tonatzuli*, do greedily feed upon: These Birds, whereof there are great numbers in the Woods which lie round about this Mountain, were so accustomed to find these Treatments which were prepar'd for them in that place, that they fail'd not to come there in great companies as soon as the Assembly was retir'd.

While the Priests continu'd burning the perfume, and celebrating the praises of the Sun, the People who were upon the Mountain having made several bowings at the rising of the Sun, entertain'd themselves afterwards in some kinds of recreation, dances, and songs, which they sung in honour of him; and afterwards sitting down on the grass, every one fell to what he had brought along with him for his *Viaticum*.

Thus they continu'd there till noon; but when it came

neer that time, the Priests, quitting the gate of the Temple, went into the body of it, and disposing themselves about the Altar, which stood in the midst, they began to sing afresh: Then as soon as the Sun began to cast his golden beams on the border of the opening or Lanthorn, under which the Altar was erected, they put Incense and other perfumes upon the fire which they had kindled the night before, and very carefully kept in upon that Altar: Having ended their Songs, and consum'd all their Perfumes, they all retir'd to the entrance of the Temple, before the Gate, excepting only six, who remain'd neer the Altar; and while those who stood at the entrance lift up their Voices more then ordinary, the others who remain'd at the Altar let go out of their hands, at the same time, every one six of the *Tonatzuli*, which they had brough thither, and kept in Cages for that purpose: These Birds having flown about the Temple, and finding the entrance possessed by the Priests, who were at the Gate with Boughs in their hands, and frighted them with their Voices, took their flight out at the open place in the midst of the Temple; and after they had flown about a while, the Assembly which was upon the Mountain entertain'd them with loud cries of rejoycing, as accounting them to have put a period to the Ceremony, and looking on them as the Children and Messengers of the Sun, they immediately got into the Woods.

As soon as these Birds were gone the people march'd down in order from the Mountain, and passing neer the Temple, the Priests, who were still in their Office, caus'd them to enter into it; and after they had washed their hands and their faces in the Fountain, they order'd them to go out at the same entrance, which was divided by a small partition, purposely made there to prevent confusion and disorder: Then at their coming out they took another way, which led them into the Road that conducted to the Mountain, and was the same by which they had ascended; and so every one made towards his own home.

The poor, whereof the Priests had a Catalogue, staid till

all the rest were gone, and receiv'd from their hands the Garments, and all the other Presents which the rich had made to the Sun, to be distributed among them; which done, all left the Mountain, and there was an end of the Ceremony.

But now, since the greatest and most considerable part of the people who are Inhabitants of the Provinces of *Bemarin* and *Matica*, and particularly the King and City of *Melilot*, have embraced the Christian Religion, this Mountain and its Temple are not much frequented, unless it be out of curiosity: Nor does the King permit his Subjects of other Provinces, who have receiv'd Baptism, to go up thither to perform their Sacrifices and all their ancient Superstitions.

They believ'd the immortality of the Soul; but they had so disguis'd this Truth with Fables, that it was in a manner smother'd thereby. They embalm'd the bodies of their deceased Relations with several sorts of Gums and Aromatical Drugs, which had the virtue of preserving them from corruption; and after they had kept them sometimes above a year in their houses, they buried them in their Gardens, or in the neighbouring Forests, with great lamentations and ceremonies. They shew to this day at the foot of the pleasant Mountain of *Olaimi*, the Sepulchres of several of their Kings, which are cut in the Rock; there is planted before every one of them a fair Cedar, for the better observation of the place, and more exact continuance of their memories.

The practice of mummification among the ancestors of the Creek Indians is completely unknown to anthropologists. Archaeologists have discovered buried remains in seated positions and also bundles of bones, which they suspected were re-buried from charnel temples, but display of mummified bodies was never considered. Copal is a cousin of frankincense and could be used in the mummification process. The governor of the Roanoke Island Colony, John White, painted a Siouan charnel temple on the coast of North Carolina, in which cadavers were being smoked. There was no mention of herbs in White's commentary.

Several cultures in the Andes also had the custom of mummifying and displaying their leaders. The custom began around 5000 BC among the Chinchorro People. The Incas would carry their mummified leaders on litters for several years after their death.

To make a greater expression of their mourning, and to show how much they bewail'd the death of their Friends and Kindred, they cut off some part of their hair; but when any King died they shav'd the whole head, and suffer'd not their hair to grow again, till they had bewail'd him for the space of fifteen months.

The Knowledge which the *Apalachites* have of God, they have attain'd to by several degrees: For, to go to the bottom of the business, it is about an Age since that the first seeds of Christian Religion were sown in that part of *Florida*, by a *French* Colony consisting of several Persons of Quality, which was brought thither and establish'd there by one Captain *Ribauld*, in the time of *Charles* the Ninth King of France: The first thing he did was to build a Fort, which he named *Carolina*, in honour of His Christian Majesty: He impos'd also on the Capes, Ports, and Rivers of that Country, the names they are at the present known by; so that along the Coast a man finds a place called the *Port Royale*, the *French Cape*, the Rivers of *Seine, Loyre, Charante, Garonne, Daufins, May, Somme*, and several other places, which have absolute *French* names, and consequently are a manifest argument that the said Nation have heretofore had some command there.

But what is more worth observation, and conduces more to our purpose, is, that at this first Expedition for *Florida*, there went along with the Adventurers two Learned and Religious Persons, who immediately upon their arrival in the Country made it their business, by all sorts of good offices, to insinuate themselves into the affections of the Inhabitants, and to learn their Language, that so they might give them some knowledge of God, and the sacred mysteries of his Gospel. The Memorials which Captain *Ribauld* left behind him as to that particular, shew how that the King *Saturiova*, who govern'd the Quarter where the *French* had establish'd themselves, and who had for Vassals to him several little Kings and Princes who were his Neighbours, receiv'd those Preachers very kindly, and recommended it to all his Subjects, that they should have a singular esteem for them; so that the affection those poor people bore them, and the fidelity and zeal the others express'd for the advancement of their Conversion, rais'd even then very great hopes that the work of the Lord would prosper in their hands, and that that little portion of his Vineyard being carefully dress'd, would in time bring forth many good and precious fruits, to the praise of his grace.

These happy beginnings and first-fruits of the Gospel of our Saviour *Jesus*, were afterwards augmented and advanc'd by the cares of Monsieur the Admiral *de Coligny*, who gave a Commission to one *de Laudoniere*, to carry over thither a considerable supply of Soldiers and all sorts of Tradesmen, which arriv'd in the year One thousand five hundred sixty and four: But these last Adventurers had hardly taken the air in the Country after their arrival thither, ere the *Spaniard*, who imagines that all *America* belongs to him, and who hath ever been jealous of the *French* Nation, made his advantage of the disorders which were then in that Country, to travers the generous designs of the Directors of that hopeful Colony, and smother it as 'twere in the Cradle: To that purpose he sent thither *Peter Melandez* with six great ships full of men and ammunition, who fell upon it on the nineteenth of September, MDLXV.

Monsieur *de Laudoniere* and Captain *Ribauld*, who had

not long before brought the Colony a small recruit of men, considering that it would be madness to think to oppose such a powerful force, resolv'd, with the advice of most of the Officers, to capitulate and deliver up the place to the stronger party, upon such honorable conditions as people besieg'd are wont to demand. *Peter Melandez* granted them most of the Articles they had propos'd; but as soon as he was got into the Fort, and had secur'd the Guards, he broke the promise he had made them, and violating the Law of Nations, he cruelly massacred not only the Soldiery, but also all the women and children, whom he found in that place, and who could not make their escape by flight.

Captain *Ribauld* fell in the Massacre; but *de Laudoniere* made a shift to escape, through the Fenns, to the ships newly come from *France*, which by good fortune were still in the Road: Some others of the Inhabitants, who, upon the first arrival of the *Spaniards*, had foreseen the danger likely to fall upon them, got in time into the woods, and in the night time came to the Village of their good friend *Saturiova*, who hating the *Spaniard*, gave them protection, and supply'd them with provisions for a competent subsistence, till the year MDLX-VII. when Captain *de Gorgues*, coming to *Florida* with three stout ships full of resolute men and all sorts of Ammunition, severely punished the cruelty of the *Spaniards*, and being assisted by *Saturiova*, and all his Neighbours and Allies, he reveng'd the publick injuries of the *French*, putting to the sword all the *Spaniards* he met with, not only in the Fort of *Carolina*, which they had repair'd and fortified after their usurpation of it, but also those he found in two other Forts which they had built along the Coast, which he burnt and demolish'd, as may be seen in the xii. Chapter of the fourth Book of the Description of the *West-Indies*, writ by *John de Laet*.

The Memorials which Captain *de Gorgues* caused to be printed, giving an account of his Expedition into *Florida*, tell us of a certain French-man named *Peter du Bre*, who having made his escape to King *Saturiova*, to avoid the cruelty of the *Spaniards,* related to him, that there escaped of that Massacre but ten men, of which he was one; that they all met with a safe retreat in the territories of the said Prince, who liv'd not far from their desolated Colony; that three of the escaped persons dy'd there some months after that defeat; that of the seven remaining, there were six were so charm'd with the advantageous relation which the subjects of *Saturiova* made to them daily of the Treasures of King *Mayra*, of the powerfulness of another whose name was *Ollaca*, who commanded forty Princes, and of the generosity and prudent conduct of the King of *Apalacha*, who govern'd many fair and large Provinces seated at the foot of the Mountains, and reaching into several delightful Vales which they encompass'd; that they importuned *Saturiova*, who had entertain'd them so kindly, that he would be pleas'd to allow them guides, to conduct them to the Frontiers of the Kingdom of the last named, of whom they had heard so many miracles, and had particularly this recommendation, that he was a lover of Strangers, and that his Subjects were the most civilly govern'd of all the Septentrional part of *America*; that *Saturiova*, willing to add favour to all those they had receiv'd from him before, gave them a good convoy, consisting of the most valiant of his subjects, to conduct them with all safety to all his Allies, and to the Dominions of the King of *Apalacha*, if they were desirous to visit him.

The information about the survivors of Fort Caroline fills in a gap left in other histories of the period. However, Charles de Rochefort definitely made a mistake here. It was Jacques Le Moyne, who accompanied a group led by René de Laudonnière that escaped to the ship captained by Jean Ribault's brother. Theodor de Bry was an artist, printer and engraver, who prepared lithographs from the water colors painted by Jacques le Moyne. The two artists became friends and later moved to England.

The relation of the success of this Progress, which these few *French-men* undertook to satisfie their curiosity, and to make the best use they could of this interval of their misfortune, assures us, that after they had visited *Athorus,* the son of *Saturiova*, and most of his Allies, who had their Villages all along a delightful River which in their Language they call *Seloy*, to avoid meeting any of the subjects of *Timagoa*, who was then engag'd in a War against *Saturiova*, there was a necessity they should cross Rivers upon boughs of trees fasten'd together, climb up Mountains, and make their way through Fens and thick Forests, where they met with several cruel beasts; that before they came within the Dominions of the King of *Apalacha*, they were many times set upon by Troops of Savages, who scout up and down among those vast desarts; that two of their Guides were kill'd in those encounters, and most of the rest dangerously wounded; that the subjects of King *Timagoa*, having observ'd their march, had follow'd them for several days, and not being able to overtake them, they laid ambushes for them, thinking to have met with them in their return; that after they had run through abundance of dangers, and many times endur'd much hunger and thirst, they got at last to the Province of *Matica*, which is under the jusridiction of the King of *Apalacha*; that the Governour of the City of *Akoveka*, which is the Metropolis of that Country, caus'd them to be brought to the King, who was then gone to visit the Province of *Amana*; that the Prince entertain'd them with so much kindness, and expressed so much friendship towards them, that they resolv'd to send back their Guides into their Country, and to setle themselves amongst the *Apalachites*, since they found them answerable to the account they had received of them.

The remembrance of the dangers they had run through ere they could get into the Province of *Matica*; the lively apprehension they had of the difficulties which were unavoidable in their return; the little hope there was that the *French* would ever undertake the re-establishment of their Colony; the pleasantness and fertility of the Country into which divine Providence had brought them;and the good natures of the Inhabitants, besides several other considerations, prevail'd with them to resolve on that setlement. But the Guides whom *Saturiova* had given them, obstructed their resolution so much, and so earnestly remonstrated to them, that they durst not present themselves before their Lord without them, that to compose the difference, and prevent the reproach they were afraid of at their return into their own Country, they prevail'd so far, that two of those Travellers should come back along with them to *Saturiova*, to testifie their care and fidelity in the execution of the Commission he had given them.

The same Relation adds further, that those four *Frenchmen* who voluntarily stay'd among the *Apalachites*, being well instructed in the ways of God, left them some knowledge of his Sovereign Majesty: And the *English*, who have some years since found the way into those Provinces, write, that the Inhabitants of the Province of *Bemarin* do still talk of those strangers, and it is from them that they have learnt several words of the *French* Language, such as are among others those that signifie God, Heaven, Earth, Friend, the Sun, the Moon, Paradise, Hell, Yea, No. Besides which there are many other words common among those people, and are us'd by them to express the same thing which they signifie in *French*.

After the death of all these *French-men*, who were very much lamented by all the *Apalachites*, excepting only the Priests of the Sun, who bore them an irreconcileable hatred, because they turned the People from Idolatry, and inclined them to the knowledge of the true God who created the Sun, whom they adored as God, the Provinces which are seated in the Vales of the *Apalachæan* Mountains, and had been enlightened but by a very weak ray of cœlestial light, would easily have returned to the darkness of their ancient superstition, if God, by a remarkable disposal of his Providence, had not sent them some *English* Families, which at their arrival thither blew up that little spark, which lay hid under the embers, into a weak flame.

These Families came out of Virginia in the year MD-CXXI. with an intention to go the *New-England*, to avoid the frequent incursions and massacres committed there by the Savages; but the wind proving contrary to their design, they were cast on the Coasts of *Florida*, whence they pass'd into the Province of *Matica*, and thence into those of *Amana* and *Bemarin*, and in the last they setled themselves, and have drawn thither a considerable number of Ecclesiasticks and persons of quality, who have there laid the foundations of a small Colony. Most of those who are retir'd into those places so remote from all commerce in the world, undertook that generous design, in the midst of the great revolutions which happen'd in *England* during the late troubles, and the main business they propos'd to themselves at that time, was only to make their advantage of so seasonable a retreat, that they might the more seriously, and with less distraction, mind the attainment of their own salvation, and dilate the limits of Christianity among those poor people, if God gave them the means.

Rochefort's report of a small English colony in the southern Appalachians has been completely left out of the history books. Englishmen probably arrived in Apalache, but there are inconsistencies about this story. The Second Powhatan War began on March 22, 1622 with a horrific massacre, not in 1621. Hundreds of Virginia colonists were murdered by assassin squads of Powhatans. The Powhatans feigned friendship and even brought food with them to give to the English, but then began killing the colonists indiscriminately at a prearranged signal. The Dutch West India Company was formed in 1621. One its first acts was to evict all persons from New Amsterdam, who were not employees of the company. There were several English trappers living there. The Englishmen may have been trappers who were evicted from the Dutch Colony. As early as 1612, Dutch Jewish traders were going down the Great Appalachian Valley to trade with Native Americans in the southern Appalachians.

The description of the English colonists presents them as being very pious. Perhaps they were actually English Separatists who had been living in the Netherlands, like the founders of the Plymouth Colony in 1621. Hundreds of Separatists became dissatisfied with life as non-citizens in the Netherlands and returned to England. The initial Plymouth Colony was periodically replenished with more Separatist colonists. It is documented that some potential colonists refused to remain in New England, when they realized the Spartan conditions of life there.

An alternative explanation may come from events in Virginia late in 1622. Over 2000 new colonists were rushed to Virginia after the massacre. One of the ships arrived with the entire crew and passengers afflicted with a disease. It was passed on to the colony and killed many more Virginians. Perhaps this ship arrived after the plague was spreading. The passengers would have then elected to settle in the Caribbean region, but apparently wrecked on the Carolina coast. Most of the Georgia coast at that time would have been occupied by Spanish missions. As English Protestants they may have not been treated so kindly by the Spanish. Rochefort's book gives no geographic description of the English colony. However, the most likely location would have been the Nacoochee Valley, where evidence has been found that survivors of the Roanoke Colony lived out their lives. Roanoke colonist Eleanor Dare's gravestone was found in a cave there. Upon arriving in Virginia in 1646, after living in Spain for five years, Edward Bland traveled immediately to the Southern Appalachians on a confidential mission. His purpose may have been to make contact with survivors and descendants of these English settlers.

We understand also by the last papers that have been sent us from *America*, that, God blessing the endeavours of the first Inhabitants of this small Colony, they have within these twelve or thirteen years baptiz'd most of the Officers and the most considerable Heads of Families in the Provinces of *Bemarin* and *Amana*; That at the present, they have a Bishop and many learned and zealous Ecclesiasticks among them, who carry on the work of the Lord; and the more to advance it, they have built Colledges in all those places where there are Churches, that the Children of the *Apalachites* may be instructed in the mysteries of Christian Religion and true piety.

The same Papers add further, that though the King of *Apalacha* hath received Baptism, and seems to have much affection for these Strangers, who have procur'd him that happiness; yet hath he of late entertain'd some jealousie of them, out of an apprehension, as it was represented to him by some of his Councel, that if he suffer'd them to grow more numerous, they might in time become Masters of the Country: He thereupon in the first place despers'd them into several Cities, that they might not be able to make any considerable body, or foment any factions; and afterwards, there was an order pass'd, that all those who have at the present any setlement in the bosom of his Country, might peaceably continue in their habitations, and participate of the same priviledges with the Natives, provided they held no correspondence with any abroad, to the prejudice of the Publick tranquillity; but that hencefoward no other strangers shall be premitted to make any further establishments there.

Those who are acquainted with the Nature of the Country, affirm, that the King of the *Apalachites* hath no just cause to fear that either the *English* or any other strangers should be guilty of any design against him, as to the mastering of his Country: For, besides the necessity there is of having a very powerful Army, ere any such enterprise can be undertaken, and that the *English* who are establish'd there, are no more amongst the great Nation, than a handful of sand on the Sea-side; this Country being so remote from all the rest of the world, and destitute of Gold, Silver, precious Stones, and in a manner all rich Commodities, whereby Commerce is kept up and continu'd; it is most certain, that it will never be much sought after or envy'd by any *European* Nations, which send out Colonies only to those places, where there is hope of making some considerable advantage by way of Trade. Whereto may be added this further consideration, that, though these Provinces were possess'd of as great Treasures and Rarities, as they are destitute thereof; yet lying at a great distance from Sea-Ports, and having no navigable Rivers falling into it, by means whereof there might in time be some correspondence between them and other parts, there is no likelihood that there should be many persons either in *England* or any where else, who would be perswaded to cross over so many Seas, to go and end their days in a Country which is destitute of all those conveniences, and cannot receive those refreshments which are brought out of *Europe*, and contribute much to the comfortable subsistance of all the other Colonies of America; and in a word, a Country, which can give its Imhabitants nothing but clothing and noursihment.

Some time after the *English* had establish'd themselves in this Country, as we have represented before, the *Spaniards* (who as it were keep the keys of one part of *Florida*, by means of the Forts they have built near the most eminent Havens, and along the most considerable Rivers) brought in there a company of religious men of the Order of *Minimes*, whom Pope Urban the eighth had sent into the Septentrional *America*, in the quality of *Apostolical Missionaries*, and endow'd with most ample priviledges, for their better encouragement in the carrying on of that work: They arriv'd in those Provinces in the year, One thousand six hundred forty and three; and since that time they have taken their progress through most of the Villages that lie about the great Lake, and upon the descent of the Mountains which look towards the Country of the *Cofachites*: It is reported, that they have baptized with great pomp the *Paracoussis* of the Province of *Achalaca*, and a great number of his Subjects.

The Spanish established the first Franciscan mission among the Alachua (Florida Apalachee) around 1600. Rochefort used the word, Achalaca, for Alachua. The number of operating missions was substantially increased between 1633 and 1639. By 1643 the majority of Alachua were Christianized.

In 1643 a small group of Franciscan friars traveled up the Chattahoochee River to proselytize the Apalachicola (Apalache) towns in the Lower Chattahoochee Valley. Despite what is said here, they had little success. A small mission station was built near present day Columbus, GA. It was attacked and burned by local Apalachicola (true Apalache) in 1745.

Later in 1745, the new governor of Spanish Florida, Benito Ruíz de Salazar Vallecilla, led a military expedition up the Chattahoochee, which burned many of the Apalachicola towns. The rebelling towns then fled northward and re-established themselves in the Etowah River Valley. They remained here until after the American Revolution.

Governor Vallecilla then established a chain of trading posts up the Chattahoochee River. The most northerly one was said to be in the Georgia Mountains at the headwaters of the Chattahoochee in the Nacoochee Valley. There is no record of a mission being established along with this trading post, as Rochefort described, but such a project is plausible.

After living for five years in Spain and the Canary Islands, an Englishman named Edward Bland, sailed to Virginia. Upon arriving there, he immediately set out on a covert mission to the Georgia Mountains. It is assumed that the journey had something to do with the new trading post in the heart of Apalache, but to date no specifics of the trip have surfaces.

When these religious men return from their Missions, they live in a solitary, yet delightful place, which lies upon the descent of a high Mountain, not above a quarter of a league distant from the great Lake, and about as much from the greatest Village of the Province of *Achalaca*. Before a man comes to their habitation, he must cross though several fair Gardens, in the midst whereof there is a pleasant walk, planted with trees on both sides, which reaches to the skirt of the Mountain: And though they have seated themselves on an eminent place, yet they have many springs, which falling down from the upper part of Mountains, are receiv'd into great Cisterns and great Ponds, where they have abundance of good Fish: The Lord of the Country visits them often, and hath a great respect for them; for the most part, he hath some one of them about his person, who serves him as a Chaplain.

In the year One thousand six hundred fifty and three, in which Mr. *Brigstock*, that most inquisitive *English* Gentleman, from whom we have receiv'd all the account we have given of the *Apalachites*, arriv'd in that Province of *Achalaca*, the foremention'd Religious men entertain'd him very kindly, and did him all the good offices lay in their power: From them it was, that, during his abroad in the Country, he learnt all the particulars we are now going to describe, and which he hath liberally communicated to us.

126

In 1653, there was a Brigstock family in Barbados. They were prominent planters. After the restoration of King Charles II in 1659, some of the Brigstock family moved to Virginia, where their descendants live today.

They show'd him an admirable Flower, which grows abundantly in the Mountains of those parts: The figure of this Flower is much like that of a Bell, and there are as many colours observable in it as in the Rain-bow; the under leaves, which being fully blown, are much larger than those of our greatest Roses, are charged with a great many other leaves, which appear still less and less to the lower part or bottom of the Bell: Out of the midst of them there rises a little button, like a heart, which is of a very delicious taste: The Plant hath a little bushiness at the top, much like Sage: The leaves and the flower smell like a Violet: It is also a kind of sensitive Plant, for it cannot be touch'd, either in its leaves or flower, but it immediately withers.

This passage seems to be describing the wild azaleas, rhododendrons and mountain laurels that proliferate in the Georgia Mountains. Several colors of flowers are produced by these plants, but each variety only produce flowers of one color.

These Religious men carried the said *English* Gentleman to a Village of the *Indians*, who inhabit in the Mountains, where there is a miraculous Grott or Cave, wherein the waters have fashioned all the most delightful rarities, that a man can desire from a divertisment of that kind: They shew'd him particularly one place in the said Grott, where the waters falling upon a bare stone, and distilling drop after drop, of a different bigness, make so exact a musick, that there is no harmony can well be preferr'd before it.

There is found in the Mountains, on the East-side of the Province of *Achalaca*, some Rock-Christal, and certain red and bright Stones, which have such a lustre as that they might pass for right Rubies: 'Tis possible there may be some Copper-mines in those parts; but they are not yet discovered, only what confirms this opinion is, that they find a kind of golden sand there, which is wash'd down by the torrents, and hath a wonderful lustre: Mr. *Brigstock* having given of it to some Goldsmiths to make a test thereof, it was in a manner quite consum'd by the fire, and the little that remained in the Crucible might well pass for very fine Copper.

It is obvious that Mr. Brigstock's Spanish hosts were successful in concealing the presence of large gold deposits in the Georgia Mountains. A gold nugget weighing over 90 pounds was found in Gilmer County, GA during the 1800s; laying on the forest floor.

Rubies, sapphires and garnets are abundant in the northeastern corner of Georgia and the region around Franklin, NC. What Brigstock thought might be gold was mica. However, the Georgia Gold Belt runs immediately west of the prime area for finding rubies. There were also copper mines in the heart of the gold mining region near Dahlonega, GA, but the largest copper deposits were to the northwest of there, near Copperhill, TN and Blue Ridge, GA.

These same Religious men shew'd the said Gentleman, as they pas'd through the woods, several sorts of trees which yielded Gums of excellent scent, as also many other Rarities, a particular account whereof would require a considerable Volume: But above all, they show'd him the tree, whereof the

Floridians make that excellent drink which they call Casina, the description whereof may be seen in the History of *de Laet*. It is absolutely conformable to the Relation of Mr. *Brigstock*.

Casina is the Yaupon Holly from which the Creek Indians made the "Sacred Black Drink." Apparently, the Spanish made Mr. Brigstock to believe that the domestication of the Apalachee Mission Indians had also been accomplished in the Georgia Mountains.

There is no cultural evidence that large numbers of Creek Indians in Georgia converted to the Roman Catholic faith in the late 1600s. In fact, most Creeks had hated the Spanish since the de Soto Expedition. The Apalachicola (real Apalache) literally destroyed the Florida Mission system between 1704 and 1706.

Before the Inhabitants of *Achalaca* were converted to Christianity, they took several Wives; but now their Marriages are regulated, and they content themselves with only one: They interr'd their Lords as the *Apalachites* do, in the Caves that are at the foot of the Mountains: then they made up the entrance thereof with a stone-wall: they hung before the Cave the most considerable Vessels which those Princes had made use of at their Tables: And all the Captains fasten'd all about the place, their Bows, Arrows, and Clubs, and mourned for several days at the Sepulchre: They worshipped the Sun, and held the immortality of the Soul as well as their Neighbours: They believ'd also that such as had liv'd well, and serv'd the Sun as they ought, and made many presents to the poor, in honour of him, were hapyy, and that after death they were chang'd into Stars: But on the contrary, that those who had led a wicked life, were carried into the precipices of the high Mountains, whereby they were surrounded, and there endur'd extream want and misery, amongst the Lions, Tygers, and other beasts of prey, which hunt after their sustenance therein.

The discussion of stone walls near temples is validated by the presence of such ceremonial walls around and within the acropolis of the Track Rock Archaeological Zone. There are at least two caves in the upper areas of this terrace complex.

Several cave burials have been found in northern Georgia. Some dated back to the Middle Woodland Period (200 BC – 750 AD.)

The Inhabitants of this Country are all long-liv'd, insomuch that there are many among them, both men and women, who are neer two hundred years of age.

This curious digression we receiv'd from the forementioned *English* Gentleman, Mr. *Brigstock*, and we have inserted it here, out of a presumption that it will not be undelightful to those, who shall make it their divertisement to read this History; at least while we are yet in expectation that that excellent person will give us a perfect accompt of the state of the *Apalachites*, and some others of the Neighbouring Nations, as he puts us in hopes that he will.

Index of Illustrations

132

A Few Words
About the Text

The translation we have used of Charles de Rochefort's *Histoire naturelle et morale des iles Antilles de l'Amerique* was created by John Davies of Kidwelly, and was published in 1666 in London under the title of ***The History of the Caribby-Islands.***

The challenge in reproducing the text stems not only from the difficulty of reading a scanned version of a yellowed book with antiquated orthography, but also from a dizzying array of inconsistent spellings. Within the text, sometimes even within the same paragraph, you might find *somwhat* and *somewhat, solemnity* and *selemnity*, or *extreamly* and *extremely*. Most of the time, the past tense is expressed by "-'d" rather than "-ed," as in the word *show'd,* but there seems to have been no hard and fast rules applied to this edition.

Errors were commonplace in books printed in the 17th century. A compositor would choose type as he read the manuscript, and at some point, a proof would be printed and corrections would be made. Printing continued throughout this process, however, and that fact, coupled with the reality that different people were interpreting the same manuscript, combines to almost ensure errors and inconsistencies. Also, it must be remembered that paper was a very precious commodity in the 1600s, and errors of spelling which did not affect meaning were certainly forgivable. One example of a grievous spelling error can be found in a 17th century edition of the King James Bible printed by Robert Barker, which had, among its Ten Commandments: "Thou shalt commit adultery." It came to be known as the Wicked Bible. Happily, no egregious errors exist in this translation of Rochefort's work.

Contrary to what is generally thought, spelling was somewhat standardized by the middle of the 17th century among printers. However, spelling in manuscripts and personal letters varied a great deal, which may help explain a few of the inconsistencies in *The History of the Caribby-Islands*.

Reading a seventeenth century text is like opening a window in time, and in order to retain the authentic feel of the original, we have kept all spellings, as well as the italics which are applied to nouns of importance.

Biographical Notes

ABOUT
RICHARD L. THORNTON

Richard Thornton is an award-winning professional architect and city planner, who has designed buildings, guided restoration of historic buildings and planned cities in numerous locations throughout the Southern Highlands of the United States. He has lived in the mountains of either Georgia, North Carolina or Virginia most of his life. He is a Creek Indian and was architect of the Trail of Tears Memorial in Tulsa, Oklahoma. He has written eight books on Native American architecture, Mesoamerican architecture and Colonial architecture, and is also the national architecture and Native American history columnist for the *Examiner*. He also designed and often built over a dozen exhibits for archaeological and history museums.

Richard holds a Professional Degree in Architecture from Georgia Institute of Technology and a Masters in Urban Planning from Georgia State University. He also took courses in historic preservation at Lund University in Sweden, and post-graduate courses in transportation planning from Georgia Tech. He was the first recipient of the Barrett Fellowship, which enabled him to study Mesoamerican architecture and city planning in Mexico.

Richard is best known for his appearance on the internationally broadcast History Channel program, "The Mayas in Georgia." This pilot show for the hit "America Unearthed" TV series was based entirely on Richard's book, *Itsapa, the Itza Mayas in Georgia*. It has become the most watched program ever in the history of the History Channel H2. Ironically, Richard became one of the youngest Eagle Scouts ever while hiking and camping in the exact same area where "Itsapa" and the events of this book took place. He is intimately familiar with the terrain.

ABOUT
MARILYN A. RAE

Marilyn Rae is a writer whose poetry has been published in many journals over the years. She is also an experienced editor, and was, for several years, Editor-in-Chief of the well-regarded poetry journal, *Romantics Quarterly*. Holding a degree *cum laude* in Spanish Language and Literature from Boston University, Marilyn is also a translator and the author of *St. John of the Cross: Selected Poems*, originally published by Longwood Academic Press. In addition, Marilyn is an artist and illustrator, and has created many covers for *Romantics Quarterly*, as well as other books. She is also a composer whose work has been performed in the United States and in Great Britain.

Marilyn has had a lifelong interest in History, and became more deeply involved in researching Native American History while looking for answers to puzzles in her own family's background, including Cherokee ancestry.

CPSIA information can be obtained at www.ICGtesting.com
Printed in the USA
LVOW04s1910090914

401986LV00006B/54/P

9 780988 964853